Bicycle Trails

of

Minnesota

To: WLG
From: TJS
& JBS

An
American Bike Trails
Publication

Bicycle Trails *of* Minnesota

Published by   American Bike Trails
610 Hillside Avenue
Antioch, IL 60048

Created by   Ray Hoven
Designed by   Mary C. Rumpsa

Table of Contents

Introduction

Southern Minnesota

Minneapolis/St. Paul Area

Northwest Metro

How To Use This Book

This book provides a comprehensive, easy-to-use quick reference to the many off-road trails throughout Minnesota. It includes details on over 100 trails, and 70 detailed trail maps, plus overviews covering the state by section, organized by north, south and the Twin Cities metro area. Trails are listed alphabetically within each section. The sectional overviews are grouped near the front, with a section cross-referencing counties and towns to trails in the back. Each trail map includes such helpful features as location and access, trail facilities, nearby communities and their populations.

Terms Used

Bicycle Trail	An off-road path designated as open to bicycling.
Bikeway	A shoulder, street or sidewalk recommended as a bicycle route.
Alternate Bike Trail	An off-road trail other than the one featured on a map illustration.
Directions	Describes by way of directions and distances, how to get to the trail areas from roads and nearby communities.
DNR	Department of Natural Resources
Forest	Typically encompasses a dense growth of trees and underbrush covering a large tract.
Length	Expressed in miles. Round trip mileage is normally indicated for loops.
Map	Illustrative representation of a geographic area, such as a state, section, forest, park or trail complex.
Park	A tract of land generally including woodlands and open areas.

Types of Biking

Mountain	Fat-tired bikes are recommended. Ride may be generally flat but then with a soft, rocky or wet surface.
Leisure	Off-road gentle ride. Surface is generally paved or screened.
Tour	Riding on roads with motorized traffic or on road shoulders.

Riding Tips

¤ Pushing in gears that are too high can push knees beyond their limits. Avoid extremes by pedaling faster rather than shifting into a higher gear.

¤ Keeping your elbows bent, changing your hand position frequently and wearing bicycle gloves all help to reduce the numbness or pain in the palm of the hand from long-distance riding.

¤ Keep you pedal rpms up on an uphill so you have reserve power if you lose speed.

¤ Stay in a high-gear on a level surface, placing pressure on the pedals and resting on the handle bars and saddle.

¤ Lower your center of gravity on a long or steep downhill run by using the quick release seat post binder and dropping the saddle height down.

¤ Brake intermittently on a rough surface.

¤ Wear proper equipment. Wear a helmet that is approved by the Snell Memorial Foundation or the American National Standards Institute. Look for one of their stickers inside the helmet.

¤ Use a lower tire inflation pressure for riding on unpaved surfaces. The lower pressure will provide better tire traction and a more comfortable ride.

¤ Apply your brakes gradually to maintain control on loose gravel or soil.

¤ Ride only on trails designated for bicycles or in areas where you have the permission of the landowner.

¤ Be courteous to hikers or horseback riders on the trail, they have the right of way.

¤ Leave riding trails in the condition you found them. Be sensitive to the environment. Properly dispose of your trash. If you open a gate, close it behind you.

¤ Don't carry items or attach anything to your bicycle that might hinder your vision or control.

¤ Don't wear anything that restricts your hearing.

¤ Don't carry extra clothing where it can hang down and jam in a wheel.

Explanation of Symbols

ROUTES

▬▬▬▬	Biking Trail
▬▬▬▬	Bikeway
▬ ▬ ▬ ▬	Alternate Bike Trail
▭▭▭▭	Undeveloped Trail
▬ ▬ ▬ ▬	Alternate Use Trail
= = = =	Planned Trail
▬▬▬▬	Roadway

FACILITIES

🔧	Bike Repair
△	Camping
➕	First Aid
?	Info
🛏	Lodging
P	Parking
🏕	Picnic
🍽	Refreshments
🚻	Restrooms
🏠	Shelter
🚰	Water
MF	Multi Facilities

Refreshments	First Aid
Telephone	Picnic
Restrooms	Lodging

TRAIL USES

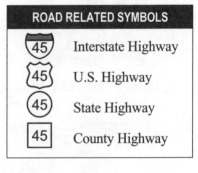

	Mountain Biking
	Leisure Biking
	In Line Skating
	(X-C) Cross-Country Skiing
	Hiking
	Horseback Riding
	Snowmobiling

ROAD RELATED SYMBOLS

(45)	Interstate Highway
(45)	U.S. Highway
(45)	State Highway
45	County Highway

AREA DESCRIPTIONS

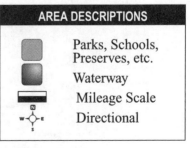

	Parks, Schools, Preserves, etc.
	Waterway
	Mileage Scale
	Directional

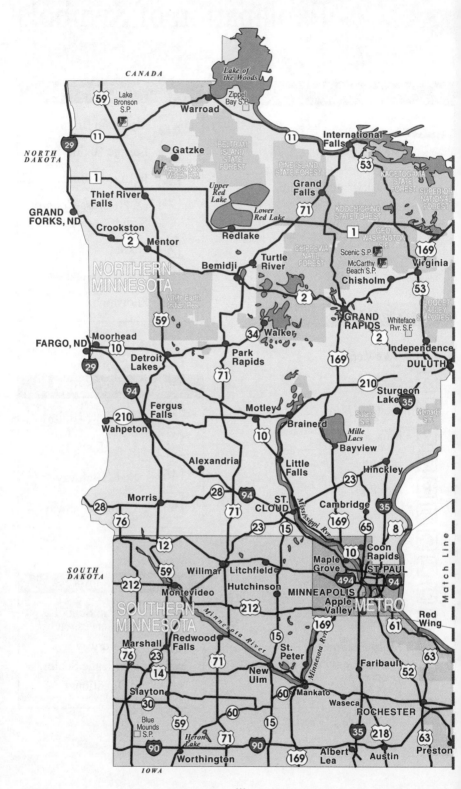

State of Minnesota

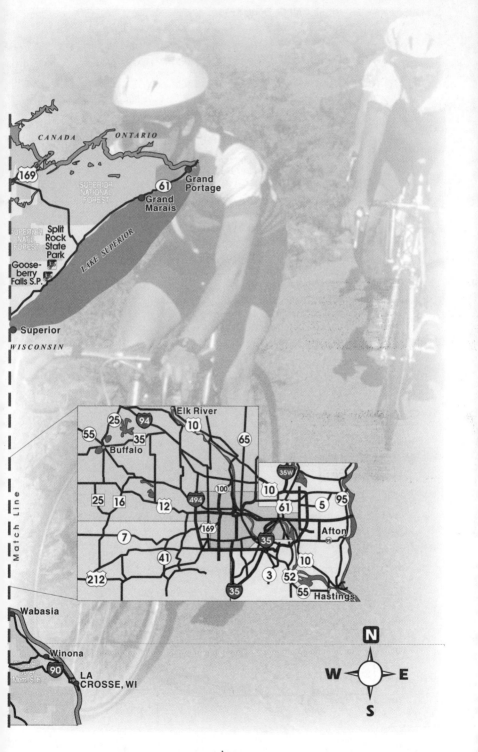

Southern Minnesota

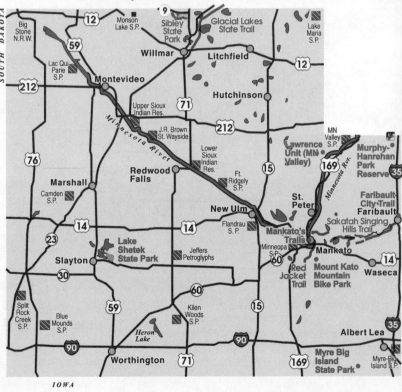

Southern Minnesota Science & Nature Centers

Quarry Hill Nature Center 701 Silver Creek Rd NE, Rochester • Open year round, M-Sat 8-4:30; Sun 12-4:30. Caves, quarry, stream & trails. Free admission & parking. Located near 4th St S & Co Rd 22 (E Circle Dr).

Museum of Natural History Dept of Biology, SW State Univ., Marshall • Open M-F 8-4:30 during academic year. Flora and fauna exhibits of southwestern MN. Free admission & parking. Located N of Hwy 19 on Hwy 23.

Dale A Gardner Aerospace Museum & Learning Center 112 N Main, Sherburn • Summer, M-F 1-5, Sat 9-5, or by appointment. Suit worn by Gardner on shuttle, heat shield tiles, stardome, library & space videos. Free admission & parking. Take exit 87 at I-90 & 4.

J.C. Hormel Nature Center Box 673, Austin • M-Sat 9-5 (closed 12-1) Sun 1-5. Woods, prairie. .5 mi of asphalt trail allows wheelchairs, strollers, etc. into preserve. 278 acres with 7.5 mi of walking trails. Free admission & parking. 1/4 mi N of I-90E on exit 218.

Southern Minnesota Attractions

Big Stone Wildlife Refuge 25 NW 2nd St, Ortonville • May-Sept; sunrise-sunset. Auto tours & foot trails through refuge. Free, located SE from Hwys 75 & 12, 2+ mi.

Alexander Ramsey Park Hwy 19, Redwood Falls • Open year round, until 10pm daily. Largest municipal park in MN with hiking & ski trails, playgrounds, campsites & an exercise course.

Big Stone County Historical Museum RR 2, Box 31, Ortonville • Year round, T-F 11-4 May-Sept: S&S 1-4. Historic boat, Native American photographer Roland Reed photos, caskets; historic flags & more. Admission fee, Free parking. Junction of US 12 & 75.

Freeborn County Historical Museum & Pioneer Village 1031 Bridge Ave N, Albert Lea • Museum, library, 1880s village, log cabins, school, church, blacksmith, PO & shops. Open year round. Admission Free, Free parking. 2 mi S of I-90, near fairgrounds, Exit #157.

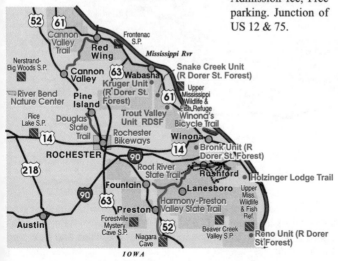

Cannon Valley Trail

Trail Length	19.7 miles
Surface	Asphalt
Uses	Leisure bicycling, cross country skiing, in-line skating, hiking
Location & Setting	The Cannon Valley Trail runs from Cannon Falls to Red Wing on an abandoned railroad line in southeastern Minnesota. There are overhanging cliffs near Cannon Falls, and the scenery is diverse and spectacular. The setting includes woods, river views, bluffs and small communities.
Information	Cannon Falls City Hall (507) 263-0508
County	Goodhue

WELCH The trail passes a downhill ski resort. Welch is a small village 1/3 mile north of the Welch station access (look for signs on trail). Bicycle and canoe/tube rental is available. Camping nearby at Hidden Valley Campground.

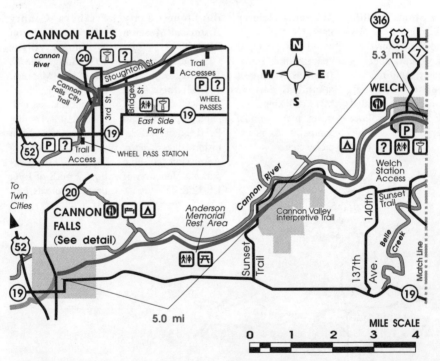

CANNON FALLS Western Trailhead is located at the ballpark on E. Stoughton St., but a trail extension continues on as the Cannon Falls City Trail for approximately 2 miles near Hwys. 19 & 20. There is parking at the trailhead, and ample facilities and shopping can be found within Cannon Falls.

Wheel passes are required if bicycling or in-line skating and age 18 or older. Available at trailside self purchase stations.

Goodhue County Historical Society 1166 Oak St, Red Wing, MN 55066 Archaeological & geological exhibits; pottery collection, Dakota tribal history. Fashions, medicine & immigration period.

Cannon Valley Trail Office
(507) 263-5843

Cannon Falls Chamber of Commerce
(507) 263-2289

Red Wing Chamber of Commerce
(612) 388-4719

Emergency Assistance   Dial 911

ROUTE SLIP	INCREMENT	TOTAL
Red Wing		
Hwy. 61	4.7	4.7
Belle Creek	3.6	8.3
Welch Station	1.4	9.7
Sunset Trail	5.0	14.7
Anderson Rest Area	1.2	15.9
Cannon Falls	3.8	19.7

MILE SCALE

0   1   2   3   4

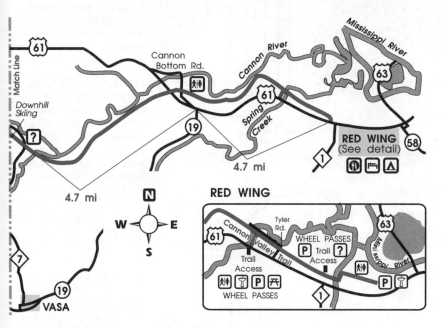

RED WING Eastern Trailhead is located on old W. Main St. at the intersection of Bench St. Red Wing is a popular tourist attraction with many antique, pottery, leather goods, woolens and doll shops. There is ample restaurants and lodgings. Bike rental is available.

Cannon Valley Trail

Douglas State Trail

Trail Length	12.5 miles
Surface	Asphalt (with a separate turf threadway)
Uses	Leisure bicycling, cross country skiing, in-line skating, horseback riding, snowmobiling, jogging
Location & Setting	The Douglas State Trails is multi-use and was developed on abandoned, railroad bed. The trail travels from northwest Rochester, through the town of Douglas, and ends at Pine Island.
Information	Douglas State Trail (507) 285-7176
County	Olmsted

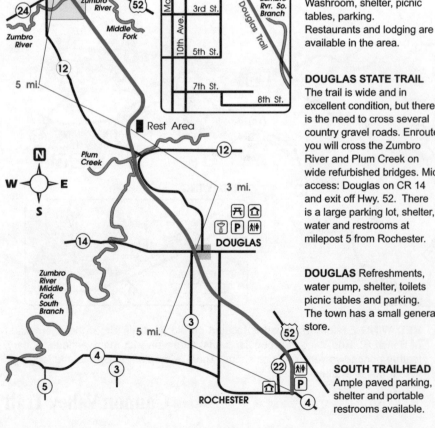

NORTH TRAILHEAD—Trail ends at Highway 11. Parking, restrooms, water and picnic tables available.

PINE ISLAND elev. 1,004 Washroom, shelter, picnic tables, parking. Restaurants and lodging are available in the area.

DOUGLAS STATE TRAIL The trail is wide and in excellent condition, but there is the need to cross several country gravel roads. Enroute you will cross the Zumbro River and Plum Creek on wide refurbished bridges. Mid access: Douglas on CR 14 and exit off Hwy. 52. There is a large parking lot, shelter, water and restrooms at milepost 5 from Rochester.

DOUGLAS Refreshments, water pump, shelter, toilets picnic tables and parking. The town has a small general store.

SOUTH TRAILHEAD Ample paved parking, shelter and portable restrooms available.

Faribault City Trails

Trail Length	4.0 miles
Surface	Paved
Uses	Leisure bicycling, in-line skating, hiking
Location & Setting	This 4 mile paved trail follows the Straight River in Faribault from the south end of the city to the north end at 2nd Ave. NW, near Father Slevin Park. Faribault is located at the east end of Sakatah Singing Hills State Trail in south central Minnesota.
Information	Faribault Parks & Recreation (507) 332-6112
County	Rice

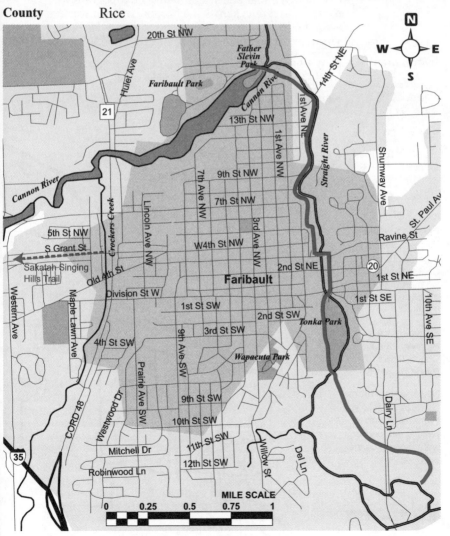

Glacial Lakes State Trail

Trail Length	36.0 miles (includes 18 miles planned)
Surface	Asphalt: 12 miles between Willmar & New London. Crushed granite: 6 miles between New London & Hawick. Undeveloped: 18 miles between Hawick & Richmond.
Uses	Leisure bicycling, cross country skiing, in-line skating, snowmobiling, horseback riding, hiking
Location & Setting	The Glacial Lakes State Trail is built on abandoned railroad bed and is located in southwestern Minnesota between Willmar and Richmond. The topography is rolling and it cuts across the border between western tall grass prairie and eastern deciduous forest. Farmland, virgin prairie remnants and scattered wood lots.
Information	New London Trail Office (320) 354-4940
Counties	Kandiyohi, Stearns

Parking Facilities

Willmar - take Highway 12 east to County Road 9. Turn left (north) and go 2 miles to the Civic Center.

Spicer - junction of Highway 23 and County Road 10. Parking is off 23.

New London - From Highway 23, follow Highway 9 north to parking and public water access on the east.

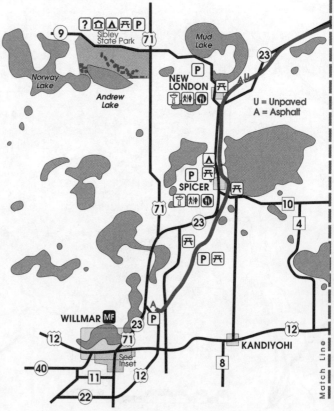

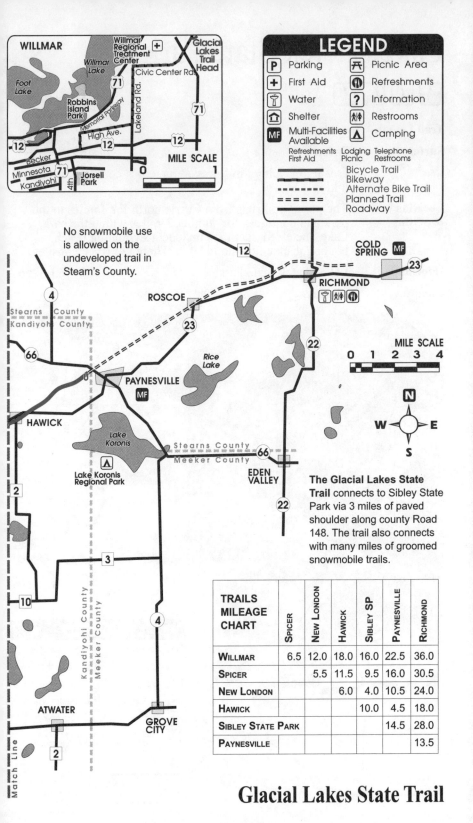

LEGEND

P	Parking	🎪	Picnic Area
+	First Aid	🍴	Refreshments
Water		?	Information
Shelter		Restrooms	
MF	Multi-Facilities Available	A	Camping

Refreshments First Aid / Lodging Picnic / Telephone Restrooms

— Bicycle Trail
— Bikeway
- - - - - Alternate Bike Trail
= = = = = Planned Trail
— Roadway

No snowmobile use is allowed on the undeveloped trail in Steam's County.

The Glacial Lakes State Trail connects to Sibley State Park via 3 miles of paved shoulder along county Road 148. The trail also connects with many miles of groomed snowmobile trails.

TRAILS MILEAGE CHART	SPICER	NEW LONDON	HAWICK	SIBLEY SP	PAYNESVILLE	RICHMOND
WILLMAR	6.5	12.0	18.0	16.0	22.5	36.0
SPICER		5.5	11.5	9.5	16.0	30.5
NEW LONDON			6.0	4.0	10.5	24.0
HAWICK				10.0	4.5	18.0
SIBLEY STATE PARK					14.5	28.0
PAYNESVILLE						13.5

Glacial Lakes State Trail

17

Lake Shetek State Park

Trail Length	6.0 miles
Surface	Paved
Uses	Leisure bicycling, in-line skating, cross-county skiing, hiking
Location & Setting	The paved trail runs from Currie north for 3 miles to the park and continues for another 3-miles within the park. Lake Shetek SP facilities include a swimming beach, boating, canoeing, and fishing. There are 108 campsites.
Information	Lake Shetek State Park (507) 763-3256
Counties	Murray

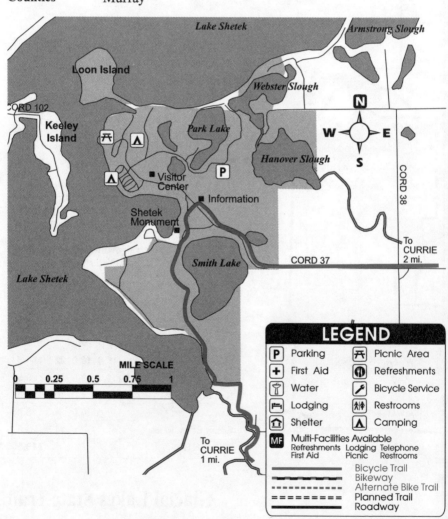

Mankato City Trails

Trail Length	7.0 miles
Surface	Paved
Uses	Leisure bicycling, in-line skating, cross-country skiing, hiking
Location & Setting	Several unconnected segments make up these 7 miles of city off-road trail. One segment connects to the Red Jacket Trail. There is a sidewalk/street connection to the Sakatah Singing Hills Trail from the trail segment along Belgrade Ave.
Information	Mankato Parks Dept. (507) 387-8650
Counties	Blue Earth

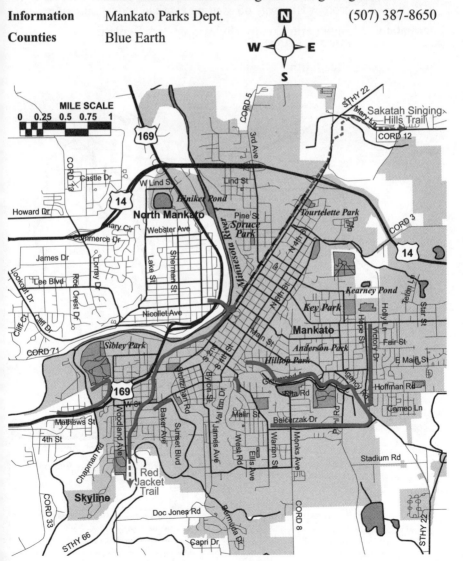

Red Jacket Trail

Trail Length	5.6 miles
Surface	Paved
Uses	Leisure bicycling, cross country skiing, in-line skating, jogging
Location & Setting	The Red Jacket Trail is built on abandoned railroad bed with its trail head at West High School in Mankato. The trail continues southwest where it ends at County Road 9 just west of County Road 33. There is a railroad trestle as it crosses Highway 66. Setting is urban and countryside.
Information	Blue Earth County Highway & Park Department (507) 625-3281
County	Blue Earth

Rochester Trails & Bikeways

Trail Length	Over 100.0 miles
Surface	Asphalt paths and designated streets
Uses	Leisure bicycling, in-line skating, jogging
Location & Setting	Rochester is located in southeastern Minnesota. It has an excellent system of bicycle trails along the waterways and through it's many parks.
Information	Rochester Parks & Recreations (507) 281-6160
Counties	Olmsted

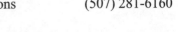

Map on following page

Bicycle licenses are required and are available at local license bureaus and at several bike shops.

Bicycle signs identify off-road trails, on-road routes and designated bike lanes.

Bicycle parking racks are provided in most municipal lots and at various locations in the downtown area.

Rochester Area Attractions

Heritage House of Rochester 225 First Av NW Rochester, MN 55903 • Located in Central Park, an 1856 town square. Exhibits life of midwestern family 150 years ago, restored house authentically furnished with antiques, quilts, dolls, garden, etc.

Olmsted County History Center 1195 Co Rd 22 SW, Rochester, MN 55902 • History of Rochester and surrounding area; research library/archives with over 600,000 maps, photographs, diaries, etc. relating primarily to Olmsted County and southeastern MN

BIKE ROUTE SIGNS identify on-road routes usually connecting or leading to off-road facilities.

BIKE PATH SIGNS identify off-road facilities.

BIKE LANE SIGNS identify a designated lane for bicycles usually on the right side of the roadway.

21

Rochester Trails & Bikeways

MAYO CLINIC

The largest medical complex in the world, the Mayo Clinic is reflected in it's diagnostic resources, educational and research facilities.

There is a twenty minute informational film shown weekdays at 10:00 a.m. and again at 2:00 p.m. in the Judd Hall subway level of the Mayo Building.

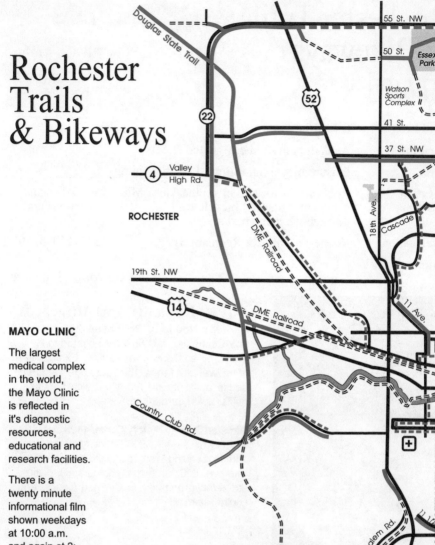

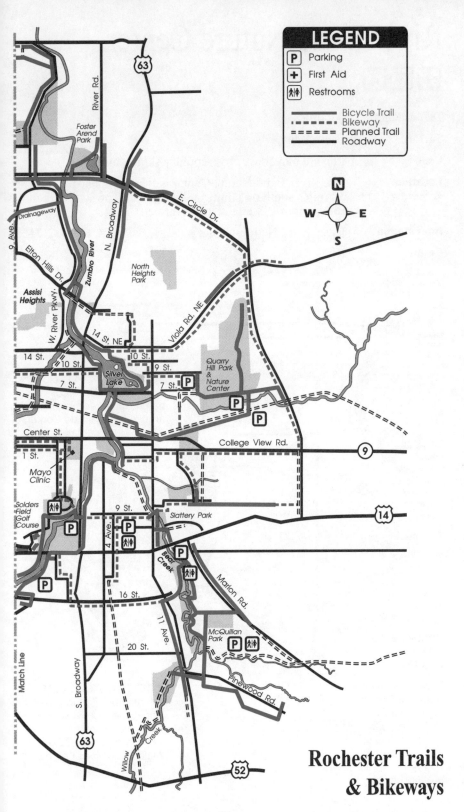

LEGEND

P Parking
+ First Aid
♦♦ Restrooms

———— Bicycle Trail
·········· Bikeway
= = = = = Planned Trail
———— Roadway

N
W · E
S

River Rd.
63

Foster Arend Park

Drainageway

9 Ave.

Elton Hills Dr.

Zumbro River

N. Broadway

E. Circle Dr.

North Heights Park

Assisi Heights

W. River Pkwy.

Viola Rd. NE

14 St. NE

14 St.
10 St.
7 St.
10 St.
9 St.
7 St.

Silver Lake

Quarry Hill Park & Nature Center

P
P
P

Center St.

College View Rd.

9

1 St.

Mayo Clinic

Solders Field Golf Course

♦♦

P

9 St.

Slattery Park

14

4 Ave.

P
♦♦

Bear Creek

P
♦♦

Marion Rd.

16 St.

11 Ave.

McQuillan Park

P ♦♦

20 St.

S. Broadway

Match Line

Pinewood Rd.

63

Willow Creek

52

Rochester Trails & Bikeways

23

River Bend Nature Center

Trail Length	8.0 miles
Surface	Packed dirt
Uses	Leisure bicycling, cross country skiing, hiking
Location & Setting	The River Bend Nature Center is located in Faribault about 50 miles south of Minneapolis/St. Paul. The setting includes forest, prairie, wetland and riverbank.
Information	River Bend Nature Center	(507) 332-7151
County	Rice

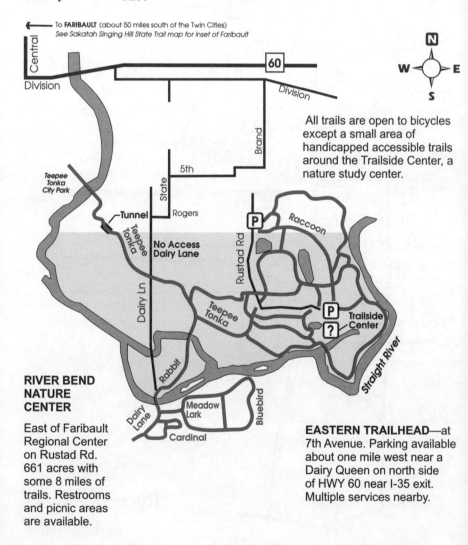

To **FARIBAULT** (about 50 miles south of the Twin Cities)
See Sakatah Singing Hill State Trail map for inset of Faribault

All trails are open to bicycles except a small area of handicapped accessible trails around the Trailside Center, a nature study center.

RIVER BEND NATURE CENTER

East of Faribault Regional Center on Rustad Rd. 661 acres with some 8 miles of trails. Restrooms and picnic areas are available.

EASTERN TRAILHEAD—at 7th Avenue. Parking available about one mile west near a Dairy Queen on north side of HWY 60 near I-35 exit. Multiple services nearby.

Minnesota offers varied terrains for biking because it is situated at an ecological crossroads for three regions - the western plains and prairies, the northern coniferous forest and the eastern hardwood forest.

The plains area covers the northwestern strip of Minnesota along its Red River Valley border and most of the southwestern quarter of the state. Here, cyclists can expect to find mostly level terrain, with only occasional hilly areas. It is largely farmland, with isolated wooded areas and tree-lined rivers.

The north central and northeastern areas of Minnesota are very wooded, with pine or pine/hardwood mixed forests, dotted with thousands of sparkling lakes. The region is noted for its many resorts and recreational opportunities. The terrain is gently rolling. The very northeast 'Arrowhead' tip of the state has some steeper hills that line the North Shore of Lake Superior.

The southeastern quarter of the state was once covered by a great hardwood forest, most of it cleared years ago for farming. The area is now gently rolling farmland, with many lakes and rivers and stands of hardwood forest. The extreme southeastern corner of the state is an area of rounded bluffs, valleys bordering meandering streams, and sheer limestone cliffs. Its hills offer some of the most challenging biking in Minnesota, and also some of the most beautiful.

CONTACTS

Minnesota Travel Information Center ....(800) 657-3700

Minnesota State Bicycle Coordinator ....(612) 297-1838

Minnesota Dept. of Natural Resources ....(800) 766-6000

Minnesota Dept. of Transportation ....(612) 296-2216

Minnesota Dept. of Public Safety ....(612) 296-6652

Root River Trail

Trail Length	42.0 miles
Surface	Asphalt
Uses	Leisure bicycling, cross country skiing, in-line skating, hiking
Location & Setting	Located in southeastern Minnesota between Fountain and Houston, the Root River Trail provides outstanding views of the soaring limestone bluffs of the Root River Valley. It was developed on abandoned railroad grade. Wildlife is abundant and sightings of wild turkey, deer, hawks and turkey vultures are common. Historical buildings and rural communities along the trail provide sites of interest to trail users. Services to be found include campgrounds, bed and breakfast inns, restaurants, museums, outfitters and unique stores.
Information	Lanesboro Trail Office (507) 467-2552
Counties	Fillmore, Houston

Harmony–Preston Valley State Trail

Trail Length	18.0 miles
Surface	Asphalt
Uses	Leisure bicycling, cross country skiing, in-line skating, hiking
Location & Setting	The trail connects the communities of Harmony and Preston with the Root River Trail. The northern two-thirds of the Harmony— Preston Valley State Trail will follow and or cross Watson Creek, the South Branch of the Root River, and Camp Creek, passing through a variety of wooded areas and farmland on an abandoned railroad grade. The southern third of the trail between Preston and Harmony will climb out of the valley and travel along a ridge line between valleys.
Information	Historic Bluff Country (800) 428-2030
County	Fillmore

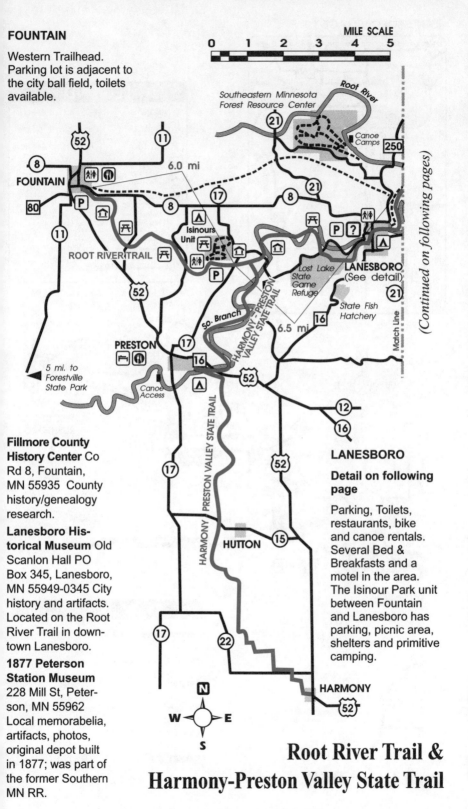

FOUNTAIN

Western Trailhead. Parking lot is adjacent to the city ball field, toilets available.

MILE SCALE
0 1 2 3 4 5

Southeastern Minnesota Forest Resource Center

Root River

Canoe Camps

250

6.0 mi

FOUNTAIN

Isinours Unit

ROOT RIVER TRAIL

Lost Lake State Game Refuge

LANESBORO (See detail)

State Fish Hatchery

So. Branch

HARMONY - PRESTON VALLEY STATE TRAIL

6.5 mi

PRESTON

5 mi. to Forestville State Park

Canoe Access

(Continued on following pages)

Match Line

Fillmore County History Center Co Rd 8, Fountain, MN 55935 County history/genealogy research.

Lanesboro Historical Museum Old Scanlon Hall PO Box 345, Lanesboro, MN 55949-0345 City history and artifacts. Located on the Root River Trail in downtown Lanesboro.

1877 Peterson Station Museum 228 Mill St, Peterson, MN 55962 Local memorabelia, artifacts, photos, original depot built in 1877; was part of the former Southern MN RR.

HARMONY - PRESTON VALLEY STATE TRAIL

HUTTON

LANESBORO

Detail on following page

Parking, Toilets, restaurants, bike and canoe rentals. Several Bed & Breakfasts and a motel in the area. The Isinour Park unit between Fountain and Lanesboro has parking, picnic area, shelters and primitive camping.

N
W   E
S

HARMONY

Root River Trail & Harmony-Preston Valley State Trail

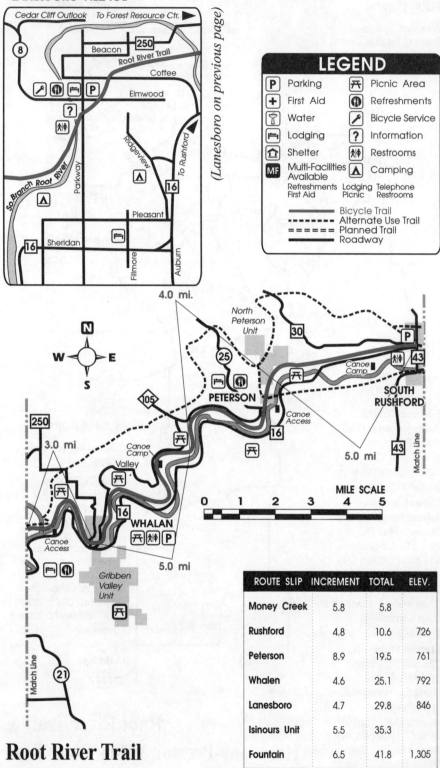

Root River Trail

LANESBORO VILLAGE

(Lanesboro on previous page)

LEGEND

P	Parking	🛈 Picnic Area	
First Aid		Refreshments	
Water		Bicycle Service	
Lodging		? Information	
Shelter		Restrooms	
MF	Multi-Facilities Available	Camping	

Refreshments / First Aid / Lodging / Picnic / Telephone / Restrooms

—————— Bicycle Trail
- - - - - - Alternate Use Trail
====== Planned Trail
—————— Roadway

MILE SCALE
0 1 2 3 4 5

ROUTE SLIP	INCREMENT	TOTAL	ELEV.
Money Creek	5.8	5.8	
Rushford	4.8	10.6	726
Peterson	8.9	19.5	761
Whalen	4.6	25.1	792
Lanesboro	4.7	29.8	846
Isinours Unit	5.5	35.3	
Fountain	6.5	41.8	1,305

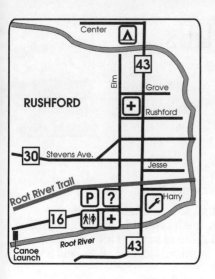

RUSHFORD Parking, toilets, restaurants, picnic area and canoe rentals near the old train depot at the trailhead. There are 46 bridges along the Root River Trail; one is approximately 500 feet long. In addition to biking, there is ample opportunities for canoeing or fishing.

PARKING AVAILABLE AT:

Fountain From Highway 52 take County Road 8 about one mile to parking lot by city park/softball field.

Preston Highway 52 to Fillmore St. (same as Co. 12), approximately 1/2 mile to the parking lot.

Lanesboro Parking is along streets, at the parking lot by the Community Center and Sylvan Park. Overflow parking is being developed by the softball field.

Rushford From Highway 16, turn north on Elm Street, go one block Parking lot is by depot.

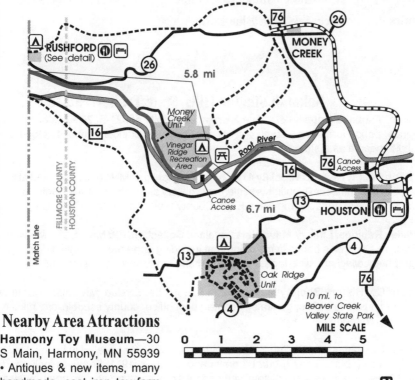

There is no fee for state trail use.

Nearby Area Attractions

Harmony Toy Museum—30 S Main, Harmony, MN 55939 • Antiques & new items, many handmade, cast iron toy farm machinery, trains.

Historic Forestville—Rt 2 Box 126, Preston, MN 55965 • Village restored to 1899; store/post office, Thomas J. Meighen's residence; costumed guides depicting daily lives.

Root River Trail

Sakatah Singing Hills State Trail

Trail Length	39.0 miles
Surface	Asphalt
Uses	Leisure bicycling, cross country skiing, in-line skating
Location & Setting	The Sakatah Singing Hills Trails is located between Mankato and Faribault in south central Minnesota It was developed on abandoned railroad grade. This level trail wanders along pastures, farmland, several lakes, and a forested park.
Information	Sakatah Singing Hills Trail (507) 267-4774 Mankato Chamber of Commerce (507) 345-4519
Counties	Rice, LeSueur, Blue Earth

Sakatah Singing Hills State Trail Area Attractions

Alexander Faribault House 121st Ave NE, Faribault, MN 55021-5226 • Historic 1853 residence, period furnishings, some original belongings; Alexander Faribault helped establish Minnesota as a state.

Blue Earth County Historical Society 416 Cherry St., Mankato, MN 56001 Located at the Heritage Center; museum hightlights settlement, history and culture of Blue Earth County and Mankato, with artifacts from Blue Earth County Historical Society Collection.

MN Valley Regional Library-Maud Hart Lovelace Collection 100 Main St E., Mankato, MN 56001 • Children's books items of interest including large mural, original drawings, autographed collection, slide-tape presentation and many items of memorabilia.

Le Sueur Cty History Society Museum 2nd & Frank St., Elysian, MN 56028 • County history; famous area artists; genealogy center; post office, county schoolroom, military exhibit, church room.

Le Sueur City Museum 709 2nd St N., Le Sueur, MN 56058 • Located in the old Union School building, built in 1872, burned down and rebuilt in 1911. Features include 75 years of Green Giant Company history; veterinary office with pharmacy, old hotel, musical instruments, paintings by local artists, high school class photos, family research center, agricultural & military exhibits.

R. D. Hubbard House 606 Broad St S., Mankato, MN 56001 Victorian 1871 Second Empire mansion, carriage house, formal gardens.

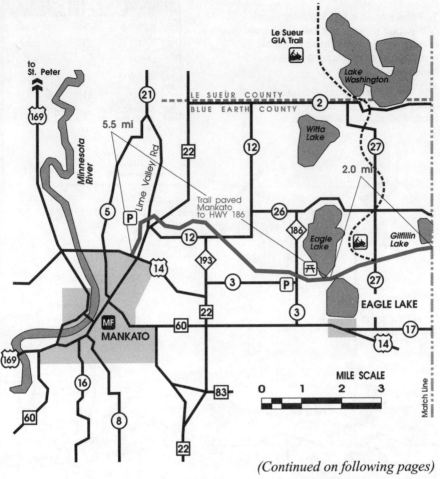

(Continued on following pages)

Western Trailhead is in Mankato. The trail proceeds south under HWY 14 for some three blocks before it ends near the intersection of HWY 14 and HWY 22. There are ample facilities throughout Mankato.

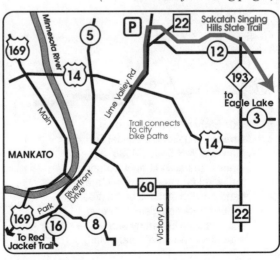

Sakatah Singing Hills State Trail

The trail parallels HWY 60 just north of the road as you proceed west from Elysian. Food and lodging available in town. Parking, picnic area, and shelter available in park.

The town of Madison Lake has a historic station house. There is parking, food, and gift stores nearby.

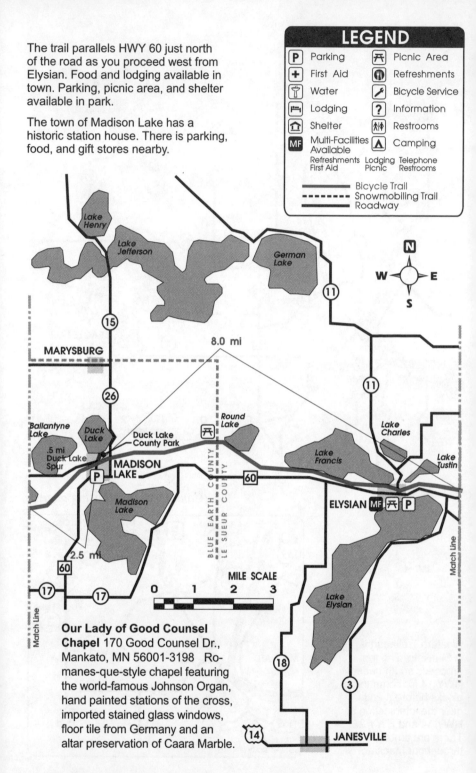

LEGEND

P	Parking	🍴	Picnic Area
+	First Aid	🍹	Refreshments
🚰	Water	🔧	Bicycle Service
🛏	Lodging	?	Information
🏠	Shelter	🚻	Restrooms
MF	Multi-Facilities Available	A	Camping

Refreshments Lodging Telephone
First Aid Picnic Restrooms

——— Bicycle Trail
- - - - - Snowmobiling Trail
═══ Roadway

Our Lady of Good Counsel Chapel 170 Good Counsel Dr., Mankato, MN 56001-3198   Romanes-que-style chapel featuring the world-famous Johnson Organ, hand painted stations of the cross, imported stained glass windows, floor tile from Germany and an altar preservation of Caara Marble.

Sakatah Singing Hills State Trail

A one mile secondary bike path provides access into Morristown. As you enter town, observe the historic old mill and dam. Restaurant and groceries available.

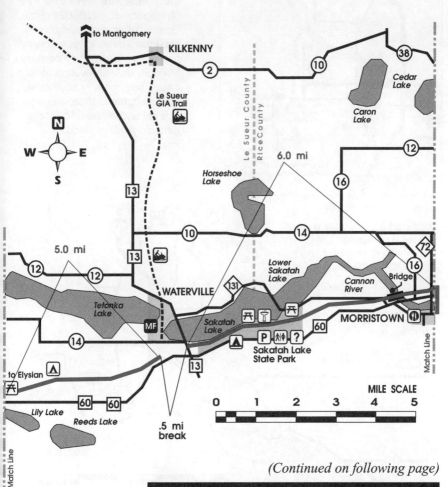

(Continued on following page)

The trail ends east of Waterville and picks up again west at Pick Street just a little north of Common St. Enter Waterville by car by exiting HWY 60 north onto HWY 13. Parking, restaurants, restrooms, and lodging available.

ROUTE SLIP	INCREMENT	TOTAL	ELEV.
Faribault			999
Warsaw	6.5	5.5	
HWY 72	2.5	9.0	1000
(to Morristown)	(1.0)		
Trail Break	.5		
Waterville	6.0	15.0	1010
Elysian (HWY 11)	5.5	20.5	
Madison Lake (HWY26)	7.5	28.0	1050
Eagle Lake	4.5	32.5	
Mankato	5.5	38.0	794

Sakatah Singing Hills State Trail

FARIBAULT

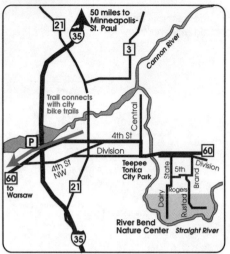

Rice County Historical Society Museum 1814 2nd Ave NW, Faribault, MN 55021 • Rice County history from early American Indian times to Rice County pioneers, turn-of-the-century Main St, slide show; nearby log cabin, one-room schoolhouse, historic frame church, two agricultural and industrial buildings, genealogical research.

Trail access near west end of Cannon Lake. Parking, restroom, and picnic facilities.

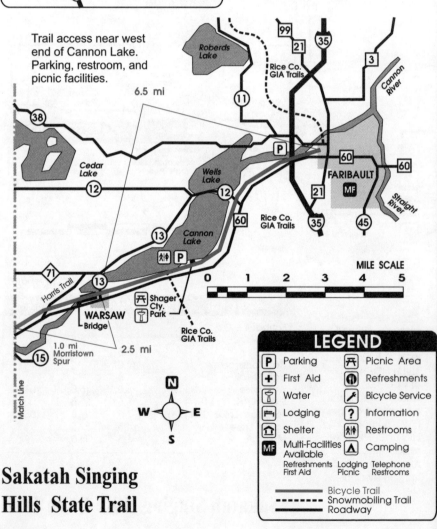

LEGEND

P	Parking	🛧	Picnic Area
+	First Aid	🍴	Refreshments
🍶	Water	🔧	Bicycle Service
⛺	Lodging	**?**	Information
🏠	Shelter	🚻	Restrooms
MF	Multi-Facilities Available	🅰	Camping

Refreshments Lodging Telephone
First Aid   Picnic   Restrooms

——— Bicycle Trail
- - - - Snowmobiling Trail
——— Roadway

Sakatah Singing Hills State Trail

Explanation of Symbols

ROUTES

▬▬▬	Biking Trail
▬▬▬	Bikeway
▬ ▬ ▬ ▬	Alternate Bike Trail
▫▫▫▫▫	Undeveloped Trail
▬ ▬ ▬ ▬	Alternate Use Trail
= = = =	Planned Trail
▬▬▬	Roadway

FACILITIES

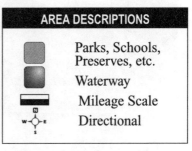

🔧 Bike Repair

⛺ Camping

➕ First Aid

❓ Info

🛏 Lodging

🅿 Parking

⛱ Picnic

🍴 Refreshments

🚻 Restrooms

⌂ Shelter

⚱ Water

MF Multi Facilities

Refreshments First Aid
Telephone Picnic
Restrooms Lodging

TRAIL USES

🚵 Mountain Biking

🚴 Leisure Biking

In Line Skating

(X-C) Cross-Country Skiing

Hiking

Horseback Riding

Snowmobiling

ROAD RELATED SYMBOLS

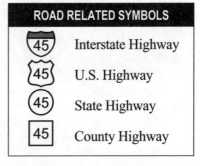

(45) Interstate Highway

(45) U.S. Highway

(45) State Highway

45 County Highway

AREA DESCRIPTIONS

Parks, Schools, Preserves, etc.

Waterway

Mileage Scale

Directional

Sibley State Park

Trail Length	5.0 miles
Surface	Paved
Uses	Leisure bicycling, cross country skiing, in-line skating, hiking
Location & Setting	Sibley State Park is located in Kandiyohi County in west central Minnesota, four miles west of New London. Exit Highway 71 to road 48, which is the main entrance. The Park consists of 2,300 acres, and is wooded and hilly.
Information	Sibley State Park Manager (320) 354-2055
County	Kandiyohi

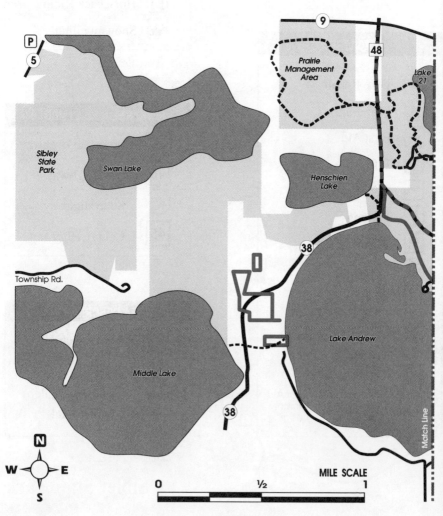

Sibley State Park was named after Henry Hastings Sibley, Minnesota's first governor. The Park is located in an area where the grasslands of the west meet the big woods of the east. Mt. Tom is the highest point within 50 miles, affording an excellent view of surrounding forest, prairie knolls, lakes and farmland.

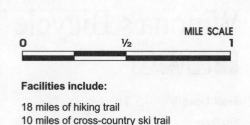

MILE SCALE

0   ½   1

Facilities include:

18 miles of hiking trail
10 miles of cross-country ski trail
9 miles of horseback riding trail and group camp
6 miles of snowmobile trail
Campsites, picnic area, swimming beach
Canoe rentals
Park store

LEGEND

P	Parking	🛆	Picnic Area
A	Camping	?	Information
🏠	Shelter		

——— Bicycle Trail
- - - - - Alternate Use Trail
——— Roadway

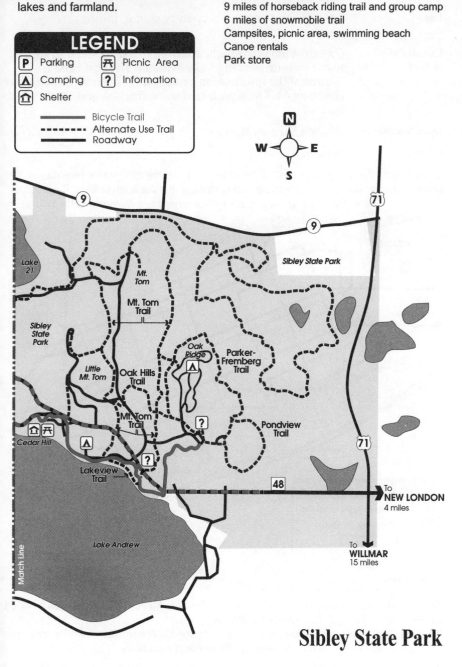

Sibley State Park

37

Winona's Bicycle Trail

Trail Length	5.5 miles
Surface	Asphalt
Uses	Leisure bicycling, cross country skiing, in-line skating, jogging
Location & Setting	City of Winona in southeastern Minnesota. The trail forms two loops surrounding Lake Winona. The trail head is located at the information center on Huff Road, just east of Highway 61. Open park area some tree shading, continuous lake views.
Information	Winona Visitors Bureau (507) 452-2272
County	Winona

In addition to the bike path, some of the streets in town are designated bike routes. Winona is on the Bike Centennial route and is close to the Root River State Trail and the Great River Trail (in Wisconsin). Bike rentals are available at the bike store on Center Street.

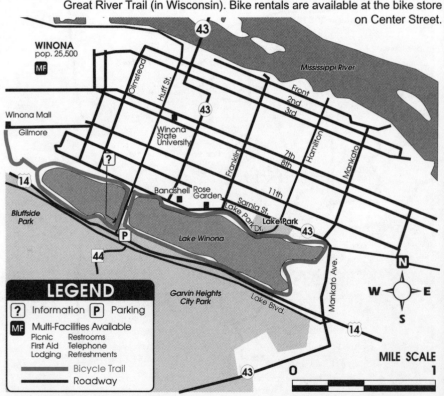

Bunnell House Museum—160 Johnson St., Winona, MN 55987 • Rural gothic wood frame home built in 1850s, overlooks Mississippi River.
Winona County Historical Museum—160 Johnson St, Winona, MN 55987 • American Indian exhibit, county history, Mississippi River history, archives.

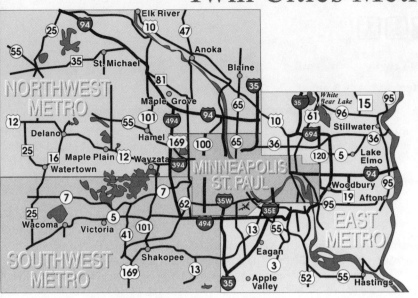

Minneapolis — St. Paul

USEFUL PHONE NUMBERS FOR
THE MINNEAPOLIS—ST. PAUL AREA

EMERGENCY

	Police, Fire, Sheriff, Medical	911
	Road Condition Information	(612) 296-3076

GENERAL INFORMATION

City Line	Sports, weather, recreation, restaurants, buses, etc.	(612) 645-6060
The Connection	Restaurants, business, entertainment, sports, live theater	(612) 922-9000
Ticketmaster	Tickets for sporting events, concerts, theater, special events	(612) 989-5151
Time and Weather		(612) 452-2323

Minneapolis Loop

Trail Length	38.0 miles
Surface	Asphalt
Uses	Leisure bicycling, in-line skating, jogging/hiking
Information	Minneapolis Parks & Recreation (612) 661-4800
	Fort Snelling State Park (641) 725-2390
	Assistance Dial 911
Counties	Hennepin

The Minneapolis Loop

Almost 40 miles long, this urban route shows off the major highlights of the city. It passes by the Walker Art Center/Guthrie Theatre, and the sculpture garden. It travels through Loring Park, along Loring Greenway, by Orchestra Hall and along Nicollet Mall, one of the largest downtown malls in the nation. After crossing the Mississippi River on the Third Ave. Bridge, the route leads to the University of Minnesota (Minneapolis Campus). The route returns to Fort Snelling State Park at the confluence of the Minnesota and Mississippi Rivers.

Route From Minneapolis/st. Paul International Airport

Turn left as you come out of the terminal, ride on the sidewalk around the south side of the terminal, then use the road between the Northwest Airline hangers and the Northwest Airlines parking lot. Follow Airport Road, then Frontage Road running south alongside Interstate 494 and State Hwy. 5. Frontage Road ends at Post Road. Turn left onto Post Rd. and cross I494/Hwy. 5. Enter the park on the paved bicycle trail, which leads to the starting point of the Trail Explorer route.

Fort Snelling State Park Access

Take State Highway 5 to Post Road exit to reach the park. Post Road enters the park and serves as a bicycle route into the airport.

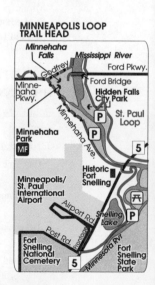

40

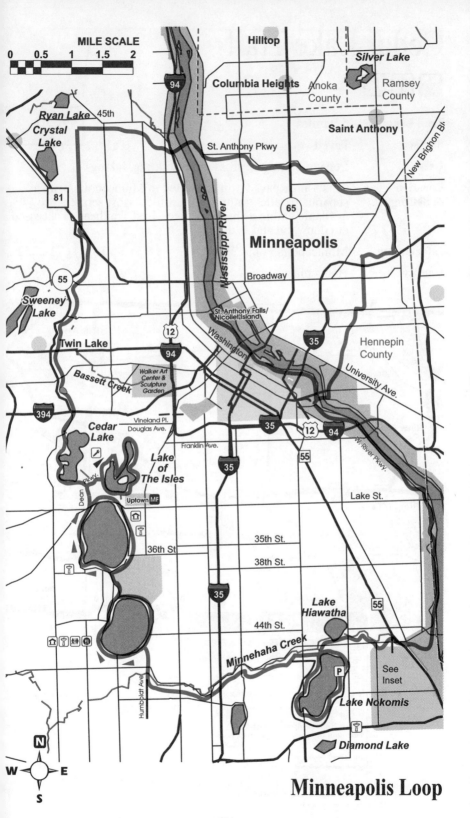

Minneapolis Loop

Cedar Lake Trail

Trail Length	5.0 miles
Surface	Paved
Uses	Leisure bicycling, cross-county skiing, hiking
Location & Setting	This 5-mile paved trail is located in Minneapolis, with a separate parallel trail for foot traffic. Most services are available within a short distance. East Trailhead is accessed at Glenwood and 12th.
Information	Minneapolis Public Works (612) 673-2352
County	Hennepin

Fort Snelling State Park

Trail Length	5.0 miles
Surface	Paved
Uses	Leisure bicycling, inline skating, hiking
Location & Setting	Fort Snelling is located at the confluence of the Mississippi and Minnesota Rivers, just south of the twin cities. The trail is paved and parallels the two Rivers. Park entrance is off Hwy 5 at Post Road near the Minneapolis-St. Paul Airport.
Information	Fort Snelling State Park (612) 727-1961
County	Dakota

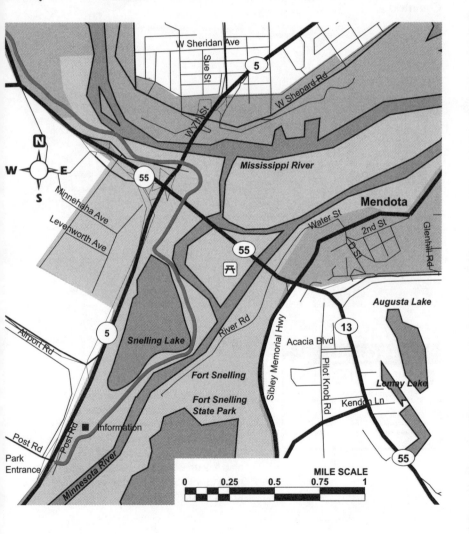

Midtown Greenway

Trail Length	5.5 miles
Surface	Paved
Uses	Leisure bicycling, in-line skating, jogging
Location & Setting	The Midtown Greenway is a long narrow park built all the way across Minneapolis along the 29th Street railroad corridor. The Greenway will include community gardens, play area, nature area, and bordering businesses and housing.
Information	Minneapolis Dept. of Public Works (612) 673-2352
Counties	Hennepin

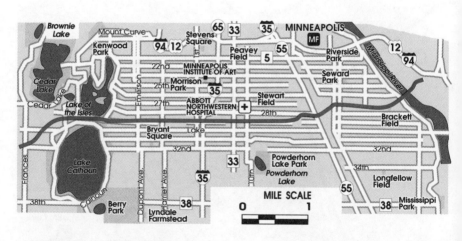

LEGEND

MF Multi-Facilities Available   + First Aid

Refreshments Lodging Telephone
First Aid   Picnic   Restrooms

Bicycle Trail
Roadway

Because the Midtown Greenway is down below street level, bicyclists will be able to travel nonstop as they pass under bridges carrying the city street overhead. The Greenway will be lit at night and plowed in the winter. It will also link up with other planned bikeways connecting with St. Paul to the east and suburbs to the west.

St. Anthony Falls

Trail Length	4.0 miles
Surface	Asphalt
Uses	Leisure bicycling, in-line skating, jogging
Location & Setting	Straddles the Mississippi River between Stone Arch Bridge and Plymouth Avenue in north central Minneapolis. Level and easy with great views of Saint Anthony Falls and the Minneapolis skyline.
Counties	Hennepin

LEGEND

P Parking   ? Information

Bicycle Trail
Bikeway
Planned Trail
Roadway

The bikeway over Stone Arch Bridge provides a spectacular view of the Falls. It was these Falls that allowed Minneapolis to lead the world in milling from 1880 to 1930 with the flour mills that sprang up along the river banks.

INFORMATION ON SELECTED
MINNEAPOLIS PARKS

MINNEHAHA PARKWAY

A parkway with bicycle trails and walking paths stretching from the southeast end of lake Harriet to Hiawatha Ave. Hours are from 6 a.m. to midnight. Park facilities include biking, creative play areas, hiking, cross-country skiing.

MISSISSIPPI GORGE

Walking, biking trails on East and West River Parkways from Washington Ave. Bridge to Minnehaha Falls in Minneapolis. Hours on the Minneapolis side are 6 a.m. to midnight and on the St. Paul side from sunrise to sunset. Facilities include biking, hiking, cross-country skiing.

CENTRAL MISSISSIPPI RIVERFRONT

East and West side of River from Plymouth Ave. Bridge to Portland Ave. in Minneapolis. Hours are 6 a.m. to midnight. Facilities include biking, boat launching, fishing, hiking, picnic areas, power boating.

WIRTH-MEMORIAL PARKWAY

Victory Memorial Drive provides pathways for walking and biking and an opportunity for pleasure driving between Theodore Wirth Regional Park on the western edge of Minneapolis and Webber Parkway at Irving Ave. North near 45th Ave. in north Minneapolis. Hours are 6 a.m. to midnight. Facilities include biking, hiking, cross-country skiing.

St. Paul's Area Attractions

Minnesota State Capitol—75 Constitution Ave, St Paul, MN 55155 • Beautiful1905 capitol by Cass Gilbert *(architect of the U.S. Supreme Court Bldg)* marble dome is one of largest in the world.

Old Muskego Church—2481 Como Ave, St Paul, MN 55108 • Built by Norwegian immigrants in 1843, moved to current site, Luther Seminary, in 1904; inquire at Information in Campus Center.

Trains at Bandana - Twin City Model Railroad Club—1021 Bandana Blvd E, Bandana Square, St Paul, MN 55108 • 0-scale model railroad layout of the 1930s, 40s & 50s, with landmarks, artifacts.

Minnesota Air Guard Museum—Mpls Air Guard Base MSP IAP, St Paul, MN 55111 • Aircraft, photographs, artifacts tell the history of the Minnesota Air National Guard; A-12 Blackbird.

St. Paul Loop

Trail Length	33.0 miles
Surface	Paved
Uses	Leisure bicycling, in-line skating, jogging
Location & Setting	The "St. Paul Loop" starts in Fort Snelling State Park. Proceed northwest on Minnehaha Ave. through Minnehaha Park. Cross the Ford Bridge to the east bank of the Mississippi River to Hidden Falls Park. The route takes you to the University of Minnesota (St. Paul Campus) through the Minnesota State Fairgrounds to Como Park to Lake Phalen Park. It then follows Johnson Parkway to Indian Mounds Regional Park where you will find excellent views of the Mississippi River and large American Indian Burial Mounds. The Kellog Street Bridge leads into downtown St. Paul.
Information	St Paul Parks & Recreation (651) 266-6400 Emergency Assistance Dial 911
Counties	Ramsey

St. Paul's Area Attractions

Alexander Ramsey House—265 S Exchange St, St Paul, MN 55102 • 1872 home of governor, senator, & sec'y of war Alexander Ramsey; original interior, furnishings; reservations recommended.

Confederate Air Force—Hangar #3, Fleming Field, South St. Paul, MN 55075 • Aviation artifacts, WWII vehicles & aircraft:B-25, PBY-6A, Harvard MkIV and more.

Dakota County Historical Museum—130 3rd Ave N, South St Paul, MN 55075 • Exhibits on county history; research center and cultural events.

Historic Fort Snelling—Hwys 5 and 55, St Paul, MN 55111 • Historic 1820s fort fully restored.

James J. Hill House—240 Summit Ave, St Paul, MN 55102 • Elaborate, 32-room 1891 mansion of James J. Hill; see the art gallery, living quarters, work areas, etc.

Landmark Center #404—75 5th St W, St Paul, MN 55102 • Restored Federal Courts Building, built in 1902, programs include performing and visual arts, civic activities.

Minnesota History Center—345 Kellogg Blvd W, St Paul, MN 55102 • Museum, restaurant, research center in beautiful setting overlooking downtown St. Paul.

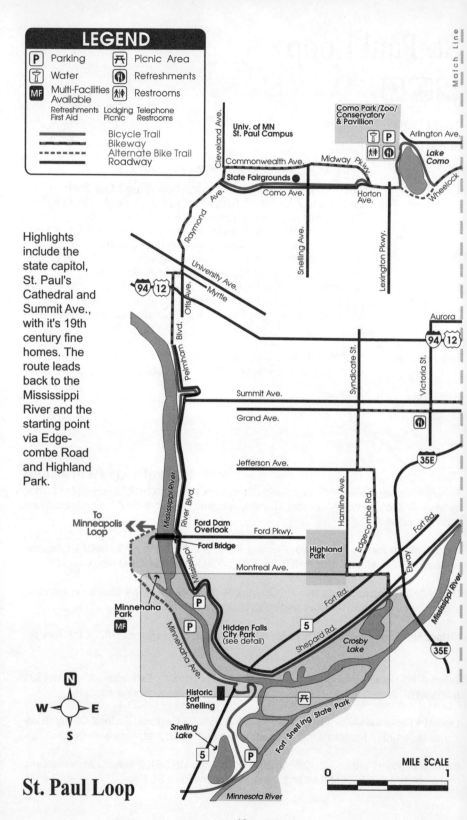

Highlights include the state capitol, St. Paul's Cathedral and Summit Ave., with it's 19th century fine homes. The route leads back to the Mississippi River and the starting point via Edgecombe Road and Highland Park.

LEGEND

P	Parking	🛆	Picnic Area
🚰	Water	🍴	Refreshments
MF	Multi-Facilities Available	🚻	Restrooms

Refreshments First Aid | Lodging Picnic | Telephone Restrooms

Bicycle Trail
Bikeway
Alternate Bike Trail
Roadway

Com Park/Zoo/ Conservatory & Pavillion

Univ. of MN St. Paul Campus

Cleveland Ave.

Commonwealth Ave.

State Fairgrounds

Como Ave.

Arlington Ave.

Lake Como

Midway Pkwy.

Horton Ave.

Wheelock

Raymond Ave.

Snelling Ave.

Lexington Pkwy.

University Ave.

Myrtle

Otis Ave.

94 12

Aurora

94 12

Pelham Blvd.

Summit Ave.

Grand Ave.

Syndicate St.

Victoria St.

🍴

35E

Jefferson Ave.

Mississippi River

River Blvd.

Hamline Ave.

Edgecombe Rd.

Fort Rd.

To Minneapolis Loop

Ford Dam Overlook

Ford Pkwy.

Ford Bridge

Montreal Ave.

Highland Park

Mississippi

Elway

Mississippi River

Minnehaha Park

MF

Minnehaha Ave.

P

P

Hidden Falls City Park (see detail)

5

Shepard Rd.

Fort Rd.

Crosby Lake

35E

N
W   E
S

Historic Fort Snelling

🛆

Fort Snelling State Park

Snelling Lake

5

P

MILE SCALE

0   1

St. Paul Loop

Minnesota River

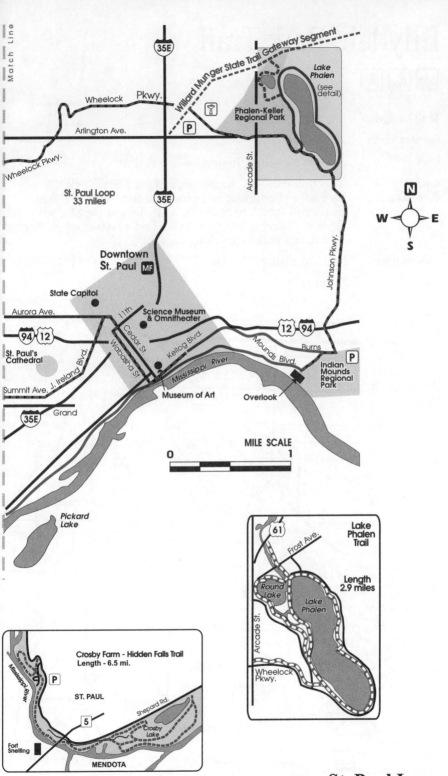

St. Paul Loop

49

Lilydale Park Trail

Trail Length	7.0 miles
Surface	Asphalt
Uses	Leisure bicycling, hiking, in-line skating
Location & Setting	This trail parallels the east side of the Mississippi River in St. Paul. The surface is asphalt and flat. Setting is thick hardwood forest, river bluffs, and views of the St. Paul skyline. There is a riverside park and a restaurant on Harriet Island, and outhouses along the trail.
Information	St. Paul Visitors Bureau (651) 265-4900
County	Ramsey

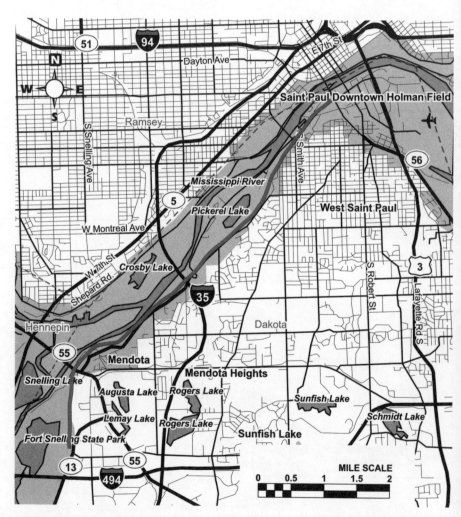

Northwest Metro

Minneapolis St. Paul Area

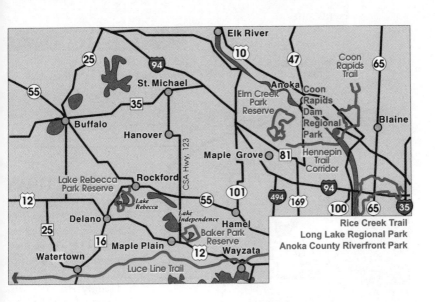

Rice Creek Trail
Long Lake Regional Park
Anoka County Riverfront Park

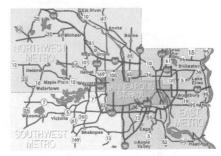

Baker Park Reserve

Trail Length	6.2 miles
Surface	Asphalt
Uses	Leisure bicycling, cross country skiing, in-line skating, jogging
Location & Setting	Located approximately 20 miles west of downtown Minneapolis on County Rd. 19, between Hwy. 12 and 55. Rolling hills, scenic views.
Information	Baker Park Reserve (612) 476-4666
County	Hennepin

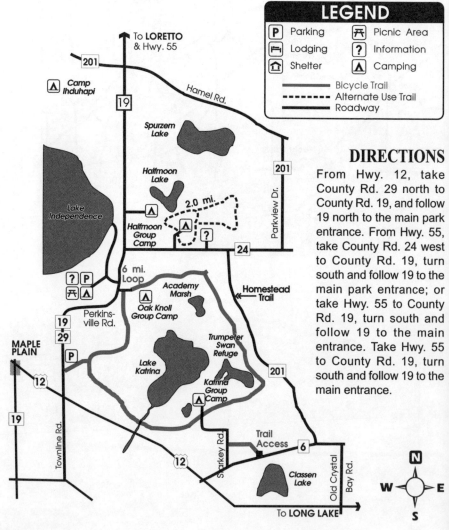

LEGEND

- **P** Parking
- **⌂** Shelter
- **Lodging**
- **?** Information
- **⚏** Picnic Area
- **▲** Camping
- Bicycle Trail
- - - - - Alternate Use Trail
- Roadway

DIRECTIONS

From Hwy. 12, take County Rd. 29 north to County Rd. 19, and follow 19 north to the main park entrance. From Hwy. 55, take County Rd. 24 west to County Rd. 19, turn south and follow 19 to the main park entrance; or take Hwy. 55 to County Rd. 19, turn south and follow 19 to the main entrance. Take Hwy. 55 to County Rd. 19, turn south and follow 19 to the main entrance.

52

Bunker Hills Regional Park

Trail Length	5.5 miles
Surface	Paved
Uses	Leisure bicycling, hiking, in-line skating, cross-country skiing, horseback riding
Location & Setting	This 1,600-acre park is located at the north side of Coon Rapids, a suburb of the twin cities. Surface is paved. Recreation facilities include swimming, camping, picnicking, horseback riding and a Wave Pool. Access from the south is on CR 4 off Main St. east of Hanson Blvd. Access from the north on CR A, off Bunker Lake Blvd.
Information	Metropolitan Council (612) 291-6359
County	Anoka

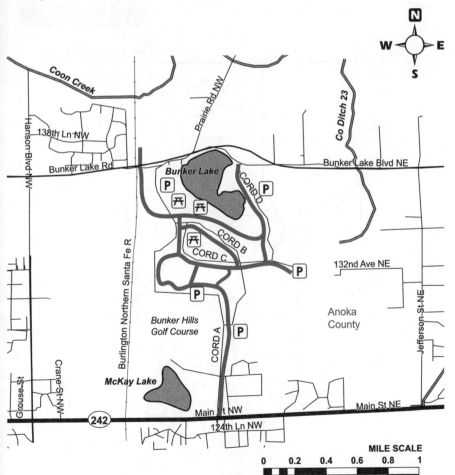

Coon Rapids' Trails

Trail Length	20.0 miles (combination paths and road connectors)
Surface	Paved
Uses	Leisure bicycling, in-line skating, jogging
Location & Setting	To reach Coon Rapids Dam Regional Park, take Coon Rapids Boulevard 2 miles west from the intersection of Highways 10 & 47, then south on Egret Boulevard to the parks entrance. The Bunker Hills Park Reserve is reached by taking Bunker Lake Boulevard west off Highway 65 for about a mile to the parks entrance. Riverfront, urban streets, woods.
Information	Coon Rapids Dam Regional Park (612) 757-4700
County	Hennepin

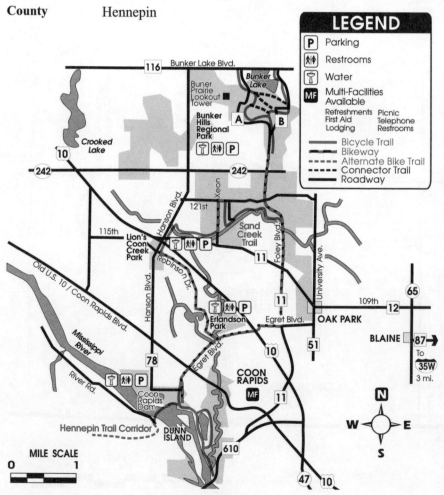

Coon Rapids Dam Regional Park

Trail Length	3.0 miles
Surface	Asphalt
Uses	Leisure bicycling, hiking, in-line skating, cross-country skiing
Location & Setting	This 3-mile trail is surfaced with asphalt and 8-feet wide. It's located in Anoka County and connects with the North Hennepin Regional Trail in the north and the Mississippi River Regional Trail to the south. Restroom and picnic facilities are available.
Information	Anoka County Parks (612) 757-3920
County	Anoka

Coon Rapids Blvd.

Egret Blvd.

E. River Rd.

1

Anoka Visitor Center

P

P

P

P

P

Mississippi River

Coon Rapids Dam

12

Coon Creek

Cenaiko Lake

P

N

W E

S

P

P

P

W. River Rd.

610

P

MILE SCALE

0   0.25   0.5

97th Ave. N.

W. River Rd.

610

Elm Creek Park Reserve

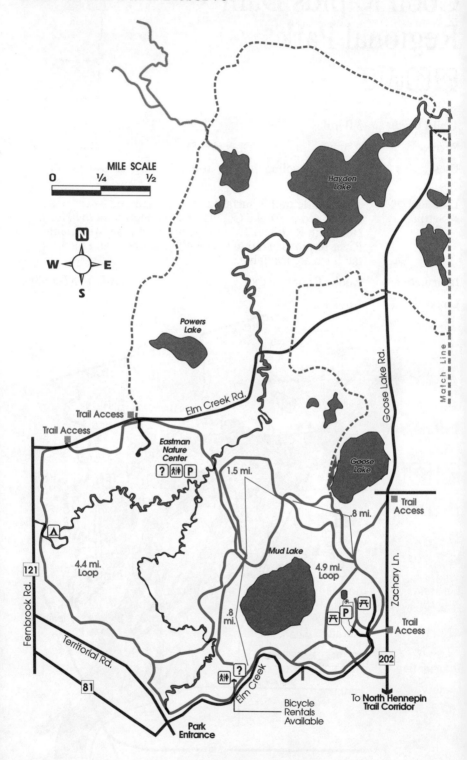

MILE SCALE

Trail Access

Trail Access

Eastman Nature Center

Powers Lake

Elm Creek Rd.

Hayden Lake

Goose Lake

Goose Lake Rd.

Match Line

1.5 mi.

.8 mi.

Trail Access

4.4 mi. Loop

Mud Lake

4.9 mi. Loop

Fernbrook Rd.

121

.8 mi.

Trail Access

Territorial Rd.

81

Elm Creek

Bicycle Rentals Available

202

To North Hennepin Trail Corridor

Park Entrance

Zachary Ln.

Ellingson Car Museum 20950 Rogers Drive, Rogers, MN 55374 • Open year round. Monday-Saturday 10am-6pm; Sunday noon-5pm; closed Thanksgiving, Christmas, New Year's Day, Easter. Over 90 different cars, trucks and motorcycles set up by decade, historic videos and memorabilia accompany each display; displays include WWII tank, rendition of 1950s drive-in movie with old film clips, speed shop, replica of 1060s drag strip. Kids 12 and under admitted free. Exit Hwy 101 from I-94.

Hayden Lake Rd.

Leman's Lake

Match Line

MILE SCALE

0   ¼   ½

LEGEND

P Parking   🎋 Picnic Area

👥 Restrooms   ? Information

———— Bicycle Trail
-------- Mountain Bike/Hike Trail
———— Roadway

Rest stops at the Visitor Center, picnic areas, Nature Center and group camp. Access from Visitor Center, Nature Center or picnic area.

N
W — E
S

Elm Creek Park Reserve

Trail Length	19.3 miles
Surface	Asphalt
Uses	Leisure bicycling, cross country skiing, in-line skating, jogging
Location & Setting	Located northwest of Osseo, between the communities of Champlin, Dayton and Maple Grove. Take County Rd. 81 northwest to Territorial Rd. Turn right and follow to the park entrance. Hilly terrain. Trail connects with North Hennepin Trail Corridor.
Information	Elm Creek Park Reserve (612) 424-5511
County	Hennepin

Hennepin Trail Corridor

Trail Length	7.2 miles
Surface	Asphalt
Uses	Leisure bicycling, in-line skating, jogging
Location & Setting	Connects the Coon Rapids Dam Regional Park to Elm Creek Park Reserve. Coon Rapids Park is located on the Mississippi River in Brooklyn Park. From Highway 252, turn west on County Rd. 30, then take County Rd. 12 north to park entrance. Relatively flat terrain.
Information	Hennepin Parks Trail Corridor (612) 559-9000
County	Hennepin

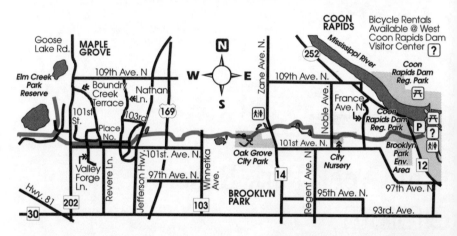

In-line skate and bike rentals available at West Coon Rapids Dam Visitor Center.

In addition to the biking trail, the Trail Corridor has a parallel multi-use trail open to horseback riding, snowmobiling and cross country skiing.

LEGEND

P Parking   ⊼ Picnic Area

⚥ Restrooms   ? Information

━━━ Bicycle Trail
━━━ Roadway

Nearby Area Attractions

Brooklyn Park Historical Farm 4345 101st Ave N, Brooklyn Park, MN 55443 • May-Aug: Wed. & Sun. noon - 4 pm. Depiction of rural Minnesota at the turn of the century, guided tours of restored farmstead, hands-on activities, living history events in the fall. $.50-$3. Free parking. I-94 North or I-694 to 252, North to 93rd Ave. North (4.1 mi), West to Regent Avenue North (2.1mi), North to 101st Ave North (1mi), East to 4345 101st Ave. North (.5 mi).

Lake Rebecca
Park Reserve

Trail Length	6.5 miles
Surface	Asphalt
Uses	Leisure bicycling, cross country skiing, in-line skating, jogging
Location & Setting	Located approximately 30 miles west of Minneapolis on County Road 50. Take Highway 55 west to County Road 50, turn left and follow to the park entrance. Hilly trail through scenic, wooded terrain. Two rest stops; water available in picnic area. Access from recreation/picnic area parking lot.
Information	Lake Rebecca Park Reserve (612) 559-9000
County	Hennepin

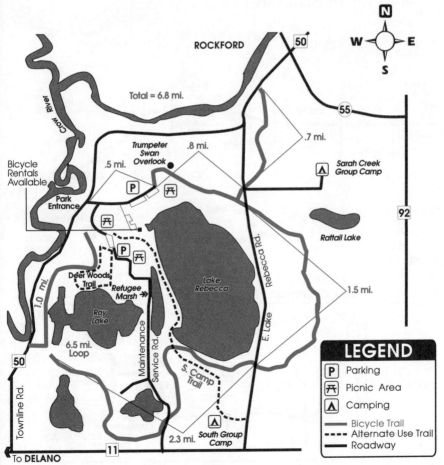

ROCKFORD

Total = 6.8 mi.

Crow River

Trumpeter Swan Overlook

Bicycle Rentals Available

Park Entrance

.5 mi.

.8 mi.

.7 mi.

Sarah Creek Group Camp

Rattail Lake

Rebecca Rd.

E. Lake

1.5 mi.

Deer Woods Trail

Refugee Marsh

Roy Lake

Lake Rebecca

6.5 mi. Loop

Maintenance Service Rd.

S. Camp Trail

50

Townline Rd.

2.3 mi.

South Group Camp

To DELANO

11

1.0 mi.

50

55

92

LEGEND

P	Parking
禾	Picnic Area
◭	Camping
——	Bicycle Trail
----	Alternate Use Trail
——	Roadway

Luce Line State Trail

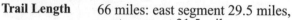

Trail Length	66 miles: east segment 29.5 miles, west segment 31.5 miles
Surface	Limestone screenings - east segment Natural groomed - west segment
Uses	Leisure & fat tire bicycling, cross country skiing, snowmobiling, hiking, horseback riding
Location & Setting	The eastern trailhead is located in Plymouth, just west of Minneapolis, and continues for 64 miles to Thompson Lake, west of Cosmos The Luce Line State Trail was developed on an abandoned railroad line. The setting is open country with only scattered tree cover except for woodlands and more urban surroundings near the eastern end.
Information	Luce Line Trail Office (612) 475-0371
Counties	Hennepin, Carver, McLeod, Meeker

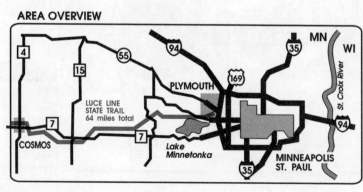

60

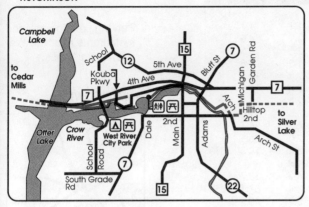

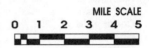

MILE SCALE

Limestone surface continues to County Rd. 9, 1 mile west of parking area. You can continue to Hutchinson via County Rd. 9 (south) and then west on State HWY 7. The trail continues from HWY 9 on County Route 85 (235th Street). Restaurants, restrooms, picnic, and lodging available.

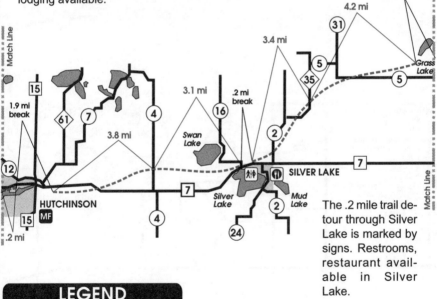

The .2 mile trail detour through Silver Lake is marked by signs. Restrooms, restaurant available in Silver Lake.

LEGEND

P	Parking	🛆	Picnic Area
🛆	Camping	🍴	Refreshments
🚰	Water	🔧	Bicycle Service
MF	Multi-Facilities Available	🚻	Restrooms

Refreshments First Aid   Lodging Picnic   Telephone Restrooms

━━━━━ Bicycle Trail
━━━━━ Bikeway
- - - - - Alternate Bike Trail
━━━━━ Roadway

Trail detour of 1.9 miles begins just east of Hutchinson and is marked by signs. All normal services are available. West River City Park offers a campground and picnic area.

Luce Line State Trail

ROUTE SLIP	INCREMENT	TOTAL	ELEV.
Plymouth			1000
Vicksburg Ln.	1.1	1.1	
Old Long Lake Rd.	2.9	4.0	
Orono (Willow Dr.)	2.5	6.5	
Stubbs Bay	1.3	7.8	935
County Rd. 110	2.4	10.2	
Lyndale	3.4	13.6	
HWY 127	2.5	16.1	
Watertown (HWY 10)	3.5	19.6	960
HWY 21	4.5	24.1	
HWY 33	2.0	26.1	
Winsted	3.4	29.5	1010
Trail Break	*1.4*		
HWY 35	4.2	33.7	
Silver Lake (HWY 2)	3.4	37.1	1050
HWY 4	3.1	40.2	
Hutchinson	3.8	44.0	1056
Trail Break	*1.9*		
Cedar Mills	8.0	52.0	
Pipe Lake	2.3	54.3	
Cosmos	5.9	60.2	1112
Thompson Lake	1.0	61.2	

Parking, restrooms, and restaurants near the Watertown trailheads.

WATERTOWN

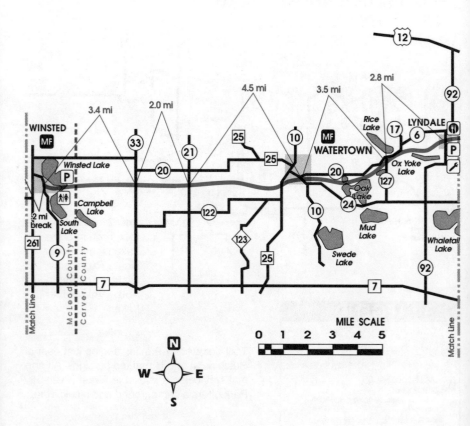

Luce Line State Trail

LEGEND

P	Parking	⚞	Picnic Area
A	Camping	🍴	Refreshments
💧	Water	🔧	Bicycle Service
MF	Multi-Facilities Available	🚻	Restrooms

Refreshments First Aid   Lodging Picnic   Telephone Restrooms

Bicycle Trail
Bikeway
Alternate Bike Trail
Roadway

East Trailhead

From I-494 exit west on HWY 12 (Wayzata Blvd.) to County Rd. 15 (Gleason Lake Rd.) Turn north and exit to the north on Vicksburg Lane. Continue north to 10th Ave. N. (note sign) and turn west a half block to the parking lot. Restrooms and picnic area available. If you are traveling west on HWY 55, west of I-494, turn south on Vicksburg Lane.

PLYMOUTH TRAILHEAD

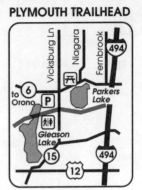

The city of Plymouth has a 1.1 mile paved spur west to I-494.

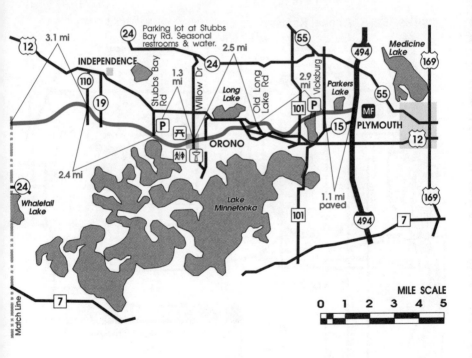

Luce Line State Trail

Rice Creek West Regional Trail
Long Lake Regional Park
Anoka County Riverfront Park

Trail Length	8.0 miles (18.0 miles loop with street routes)
Surface	Paved, gravel
Uses	Leisure bicycling, cross country skiing, in-line skating, jogging
Location & Setting	This path takes you from Long Lake in New Brighton west along Rice Creek through Findley and a ride along the Mississippi River through Anoka County Riverfront Park to 42nd Avenue. From the intersection of I-35W and I-694, take I-35W to Highway 96, then west to 1st Avenue, then south to the park entrance. Waterviews, parkways, urban.
Information	Long Lake Regional Park (651) 777-1707
	Anoka County Parks (612) 757-3920
Counties	Anoka, Ramsey

The route is mainly level except for some short grades and gravel paths along Rice Creek east of Central. There is a short road connection on Stinson, and another stretch with a wide bike lane along East River Rd.

Southwest Metro

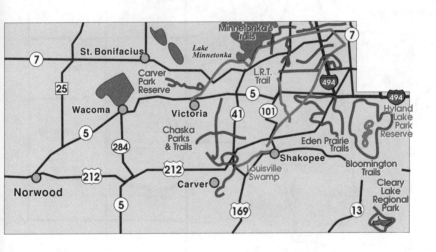

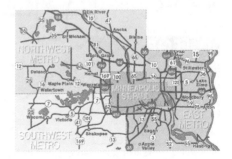

Bloomington Trails

Trail Length	19.0 miles
Surface	Paved
Uses	Leisure bicycling, in-line skating, jogging
Location & Setting	Bloomington is a suburb located southwest of the Twin Cities. A convenient starting point is from the main parking lot in Hyland Lake Park Reserve. Take Normandale Blvd. south from I-494 to 84th Street. Turn west and follow 84th to East Bush Lake Road, then south to the entrance. Be prepared for hills. Park & suburban setting.
Information	Hyland Lake Park Reserve (612) 941-4362
County	Hennepin

To Mall of America
494

Martin Rd.
Lea
East Bush Lake Rd.
84th
Pauly's Pond Park
17
32
84th

Richson Nature Center
Mt. Normandale Lake Park
Lake Girard Park

Bush Lake Park
Mt. Gilboa
90th

Anderson Lakes P Kwy.
West Bush Lake Rd.
Poplar Bridge
Barthel's Pond

94th
Japanese Gardens
34
Marsh Lake Park

Hyland Lake County Park

EDEN PRAIRIE
98th St.
17

102nd

Hyland Lake
28
1

Bloomington Ferry Rd.
106th
1
108th
France Ave.

N
W — **E**
S

MILE SCALE
0   1

LEGEND

🚰	Water
🚻	Restrooms
——	Bicycle Trail
- - -	Alternate Bike Trail
▪▪▪	Connector Trail
▬▬	Roadway

Auto Club Rd.
34
Bloomington Bluffs Mountain Bike Trail
Minnesota River

Bloomington is the third largest city in Minnesota and the home of "Mall of America". Among the sites along the route is the Normandale Japanese Garden, which was exquisitely designed by Takao Watanabe, a landscape artist from Tokyo, and Richardson Nature Center, with its many nature attractions.

Carver Park Reserve
Hennepin Parks

Trail Length	8.5 miles	
Surface	Asphalt	
Uses	Leisure bicycling, cross country skiing, in-line skating, jogging	
Location & Setting	Located in Victoria, on Carver County Road 11. Take Highway 7 west from Minneapolis and turn left on County Road 11 or take Highway 5 west from Minneapolis and turn right on County Road 11. Follow signs to picnic area or trailhead. Moderate terrain. Rest stops at Lowry Nature Center and Parley Lake picnic area. Access from Nature Center or picnic area.	
Information	Carver Park Reserve	(612) 472-4911
County	Carver	

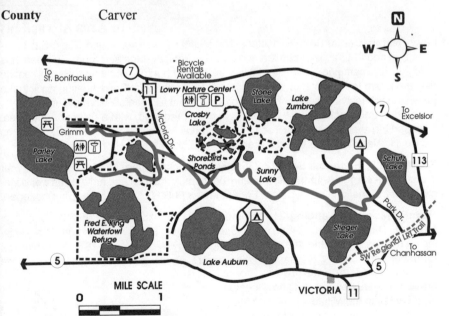

LEGEND

P Parking   **⚘** Picnic Area
⚠ Camping   **⚘** Restrooms
⚑ Water

——————— Bicycle Trail
- - - - - - - Alternate Bike Trail
- - - - - - - Alternate Use Trail
——————— Roadway

Additional short turf trails near Nature Center. The Minnesota Landscape Arboretum is nearby and allows biking on a three mile drive.

Paved bike trails connects to the 27 miles Southwest Regional LRT Trail via an aggregate connector trail running parallel to Park Drive.

Chaska's Trails

Trail Length	17.0 miles
Surface	Paved, gravel*
Uses	Leisure bicycling, cross country skiing, in-line skating, hiking
Location & Setting	Chaska is located in Carver County, southwest of the Twin Cities. The City Square is a good place to start, but there are numerous access points with parking along the route. You'll travel past lakes, through wooded ravines, experiencing some hills in addition to suburban areas.
Information	City of Chaska
County	Carver

> * The path between Chaska City Square and Shakopee is paved. The route along Pioneer Trail Road is a paved shoulder. The remainder of the route is mostly gravel.

Nearby Area Attractions

Lowry Nature Center Box 270, Victoria, MN 55386 • Open year round. Tues.-Sat. 9am-5pm, Sun noon-5pm; also open Memorial Day-Labor Day: Mon 9am-5pm. This park has 4 large lakes, camping, canoeing, hiking, biking and horseback riding trails, recreation play area, bird feeding station, 4 observation decks and a half-mile floating dock in the marsh. Also, beehive observation, family programs and bike rental. Informational displays, self guided trail brochures. Hennepin park permit required, with a daily or annual fee. Free parking available the first Tues. of each month. Located 8.5 mi W of Excelsior on Co Rd 11. Also 6 mi W of Chanhassen on Hwy 5, then 1.5 mi N on CR 11.

Scott County Historical Society 235 S Fuller St, Shakopee, MN 55379 • Open year round. Wed-Sat 10am-4pm. This museum contains African art and artifacts as well as local history. Donations appreciated. Free parking. 1 blk N of Court House in Shakopee.

Historic Murphy's Landing 2187 East Hwy 101, Shakopee, MN 55379 • Mar-Dec. Memorial Day-Labor Day: T-Sun 10am-5pm; Mar-Dec: M-F by reservation; Thanksgiving-Christmas: Sat & Sun 10am-4pm. Living history re-creation of 1840-90 settler life; fur trader cabin, farms, blacksmith, town square, shops; boat excursion, schoolhouse classes, costumed interpreters, horse drawn trolley, restaurant, gift shop; located on 87 acres in the Minnesota River Valley. Admission fee, with group rate available. Free parking. Located 1 mile east of Shakopee on Hwy 101.

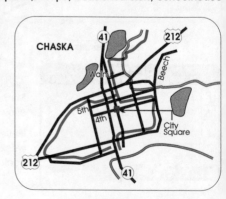

Chaska's Trails

LEGEND

P	Parking
🗻	Picnic Area
🍴	Refreshments
——	Bicycle Trail
- - -	Alternate Bike Trail
——	Roadway

MILE SCALE

0 ⸻ 1

Cleary Lake Regional Park

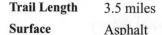

Trail Length	3.5 miles
Surface	Asphalt
Uses	Leisure bicycling, cross country skiing, in-line skating, jogging
Location & Setting	Near Prior Lake on Scott County Road 27. From Highway 35W, go west on County Road 42, then south on County Road 27, or take I-494 to County Road 18, go south on 18, then east on Highway 101, south on Highway 13, east on County Road 42, then south again on County Road 27 to the park entrance. Flat terrain around the lake with one gradual hill. Three rest stops and one water pump stop. Access at Visitor Center.
Information	Cleary Lake Regional Park (612) 447-2171
County	Scott

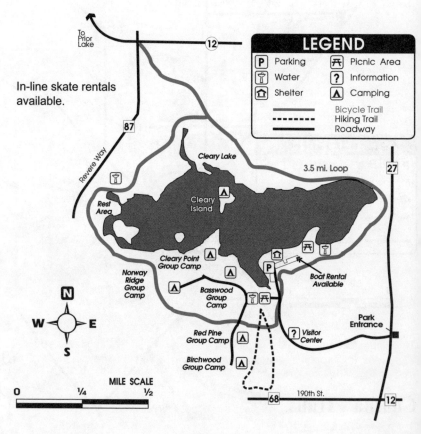

In-line skate rentals available.

LEGEND

P Parking
Water
Shelter
Picnic Area
? Information
Camping
Bicycle Trail
Hiking Trail
Roadway

To Prior Lake

Cleary Lake

3.5 mi. Loop

Cleary Island

Rest Area

Cleary Point Group Camp

Norway Ridge Group Camp

Basswood Group Camp

Red Pine Group Camp

Birchwood Group Camp

Boat Rental Available

Park Entrance

? Visitor Center

190th St.

MILE SCALE

0   ¼   ½

N   W   E   S

70

Eden Prairie Trails

Trail Length	20.0 miles
Surface	Paved
Uses	Leisure bicycling, in-line skating, hiking/jogging
Location & Setting	Eden Prairie, a suburb located southwest of the twin cities. The path meanders through the community, looping Staring Lake and Round Lake in route. The city got its name in 1853 from a eastern journalist, Mrs. Elizabeth Ellet, who described the area as a "garden of Eden". A good starting point is the parking lot on the south side of Staring Lake and across from the Planes of Fame Air Museum. Parks, suburban setting.
Information	Eden Prairie City Offices (612) 949-8300
County	Hennepin

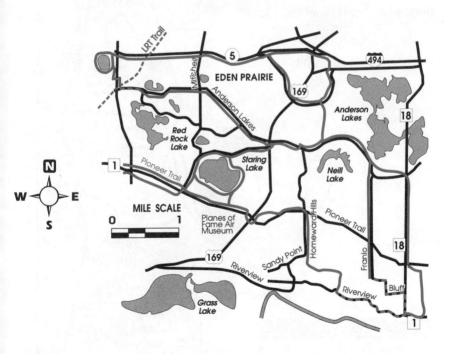

The Planes of Fame Air Museum is well worth the visit. It features restored planes from World War II. It's open Tuesday through Sunday and there is a charge. You can even sign up for a open cockpit flight in a Stearman.

Staring Lake Park — Provides a 2.5 mile bike path around the lake, and a 500 seat amphitheater for concerts and plays throughout the summer.

Hyland Lake Park Reserve

Trail Length	5.5 miles
Surface	Asphalt
Uses	Leisure bicycling, cross country skiing, in-line skating, jogging
Location & Setting	Located on East Bush Lake Road in Bloomington. From I-494, go south on Normandale Boulevard to 84th Street. Turn Right and follow 84th Street to East Bush Lake Road. Go south on East Lake Bush Road and follow the signs to Richardson Nature Center and Hyland Lake Visitor Center. Northern loop through rolling hills and scenic meadows; southern loop through woodlands. Trails connect to adjacent neighborhoods. Two rest areas. Access from Visitor Center.
Information	Hyland Lake Park Reserve (612) 941-4362
County	Hennepin

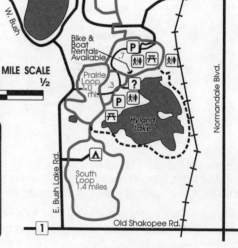

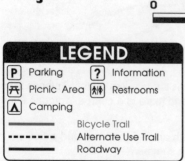

LEGEND

P	Parking	**?**	Information
⌗	Picnic Area	**⚥**	Restrooms
A	Camping		

—————— Bicycle Trail
- - - - - - Alternate Use Trail
—————— Roadway

Louisville Swamp
Minnesota Valley State Recreation Area

Trail Length	6.5 miles
Surface	Paved (plus 13.5 miles grass & dirt trail)
Uses	Leisure bicycling, in-line skating, cross country skiing, hiking
Location & Setting	Southwest of Minneapolis with trailheads in Shakopee and Chaska. There is parking in Chaska off State Highway 41 and in Shakopee at the Huber Park trailhead near city hall, one block east of Highway 169. The trail was built on an old railroad bed. It crosses the Minnesota River on the original railroad swing bridge.
Information	Minnesota Valley State Park (612) 492-6400
County	Carver

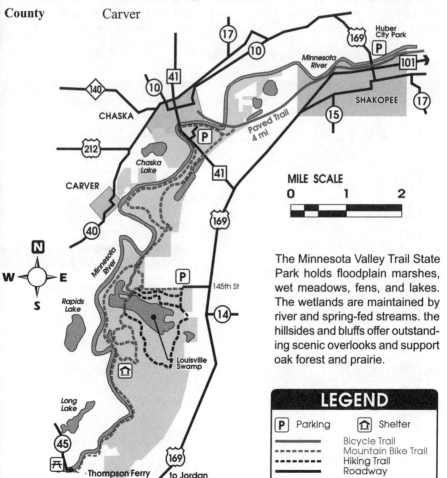

The Minnesota Valley Trail State Park holds floodplain marshes, wet meadows, fens, and lakes. The wetlands are maintained by river and spring-fed streams. the hillsides and bluffs offer outstanding scenic overlooks and support oak forest and prairie.

LEGEND

P Parking	**⌂** Shelter

Bicycle Trail
Mountain Bike Trail
Hiking Trail
Roadway

Southwest Metro Local Area Parks

Bryant Lake (612) 941-4518

Located in Eden Prairie, the 170 acre park, nestled among rolling hills is a perfect spot for a summer afternoon outing. There is a parking fee, and normal hours are from 5 a.m. to sunset. Facilities include biking, boat launching, canoeing, fishing, hiking, ice fishing, picnic area, power boating, sailing.

Hyland Lake Park Reserve (612) 948-8877

This 1,000 acre park is surrounded by the City of Bloomington. This popular park annually attracts some 450,000 visitors to its nature programs and extensive recreation facilities. Reservation picnic area and group camp sites are available. There is a parking fee and normal hours are 5 a.m. to sunset. Facilities include biking, boat launching, canoeing, creative play area, fishing, golf, hiking, picnic area, sailing, cross-country skiing, snowmobiling, snowshoeing.

Murphy-hanrehan Park Reserve (612) 447-6913

The glacial ridges and hilly terrain of northwest Scott County make this 2,400 acre park popular with mountain bikers and hikers, and a challenging cross-country ski area. There is a parking fee and normal hours are from 5 a.m. to sunset. Facilities include mountain biking, hiking, horseback riding, cross-country skiing, snowmobiling.

FACILITIES

- Bike Repair
- Camping
- First Aid
- Info
- Lodging
- Parking
- Picnic
- Refreshments
- Restrooms
- Shelter
- Water
- MF Multi Facilities
  - Refreshments, First Aid
  - Telephone, Picnic
  - Restrooms, Lodging

ROUTES

- Biking Trail
- Bikeway
- Alternate Bike Trail
- Undeveloped Trail
- Alternate Use Trail
- Planned Trail
- Roadway

TRAIL USES

- Mountain Biking
- Leisure Biking
- In Line Skating
- (X-C) Cross-Country Skiing
- Hiking
- Horseback Riding
- Snowmobiling

LRT Trail

Trail Length	North corridor - 15.5 miles South corridor - 11.5 miles
Surface	Crushed limestone - 10 feet wide
Uses	Leisure bicycling, cross country skiing, hiking
Location & Setting	The Southwest Regional LRT Trail includes two corridors that follow abandoned railroad right-of-way through the southwestern metro Twin Cities area. The north corridor begins in Hopkins on the west side of Eighth Avenue North, just north of Main street and runs to downtown Victoria. The south corridor also begins in Hopkins, at the *Park and Ride* lot southeast of the intersection of Eight Avenue South and County Road 3 and extends to Chanhassen.
Information	Hennepin Parks (612) 559-9000 Trail Hotline (612) 559-6778
Counties	Hennepin, Carver

(See map on following pages)

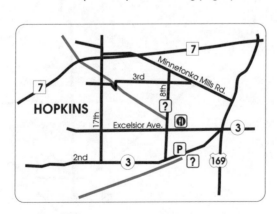

The Trails is two-way and includes wooden bridges and several road crossings. Designated parking areas are available along both corridors. Trail hours are from 5 a.m. to sunset. Motorized vehicles are prohibited.

The Hennepin Parks system consists of 25,000 acres of park land including seven large park reserves, five regional park Noerenberg Gardens, the North Hennepin Regional Trail Corridor besides the LRT trail.

The average trail grade is 1%, with a maximum of 5%. The average cross slope is 0% with a maximum of 1%.

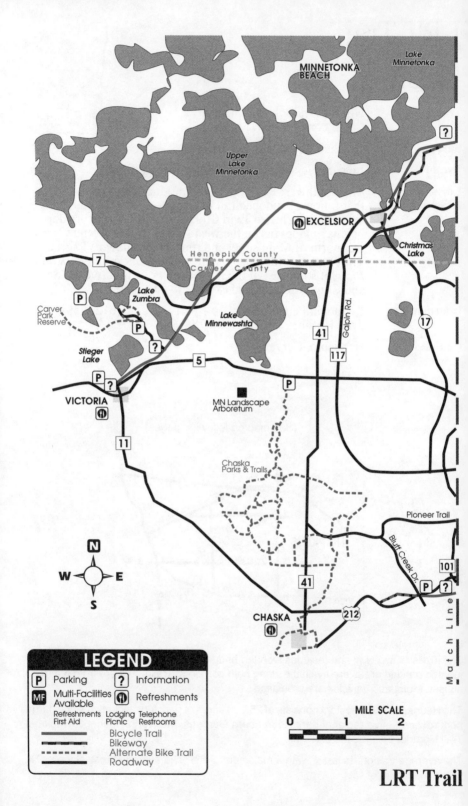

MINNETONKA
BEACH

Lake
Minnetonka

Upper
Lake
Minnetonka

⚑EXCELSIOR

Christmas
Lake

Hennepin County
Carver County

7

Galpin Rd.

17

7

P

Lake
Zumbra

Carver
Park
Reserve

P

Lake
Minnewashta

41

117

?

Stieger
Lake

5

P

P

MN Landscape
Arboretum

?

VICTORIA
⚑

11

Chaska
Parks & Trails

Pioneer Trail

Bluff Creek Dr.

101

P

?

N
W ✦ E
S

41

CHASKA
⚑

212

Match Line

LEGEND

P	Parking	?	Information
MF	Multi-Facilities Available	⚑	Refreshments

Refreshments   Lodging   Telephone
First Aid   Picnic   Restrooms

——— Bicycle Trail
      Bikeway
- - - - Alternate Bike Trail
——— Roadway

MILE SCALE

0   1   2

LRT Trail

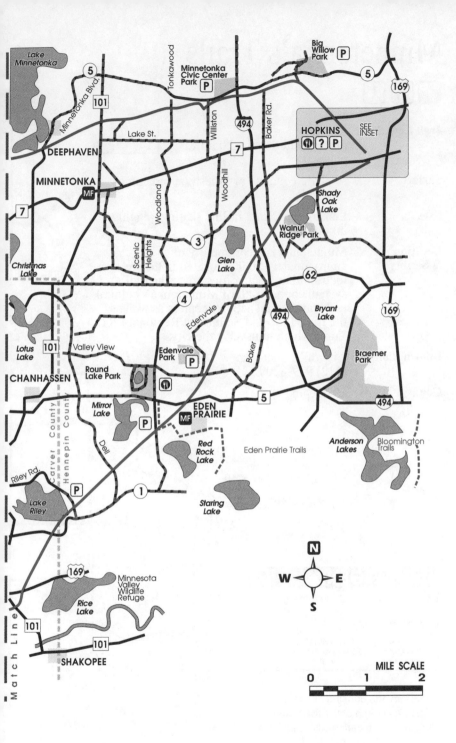

LRT Trail

Minnetonka's Trails

🚲 ⛸ 🚶

Trail Length	28.0 miles—plus an additional 12.0 miles planned
Surface	Asphalt, concrete or limestone screenings; 8 feet wide
Uses	Leisure bicycling, in-line skating, jogging/hiking
Location & Setting	Minnetonka is a community of approximately 50,000 located in the western metropolitan Twin-Cities area. The trail system connects all of Minnetonka's cultural and commercial activity centers as well as the Luce Line and Southwest Regional LRT Trails which transverse the city.
Information	City of Minnetonka (612) 939-8200
County	Hennepin

N
W E
S

MILE SCALE
0   1

LEGEND

P Parking   👫 Restrooms

Bicycle Trail
Bikeway
Alternate Bike Trail
Hiking/Walking Trail
Planned Trail
Roadway

Restroom and drinking fountains are available in each of the five community parks. The park facilities include a wide variety of opportunities such as picnicking, canoeing, fishing, skating, swimming and group sports. The trails close at 10:00 p.m.

Luce Line Trail
Gleason Lake
Match Line
12
101
16
Grays Bay
DEEPHAVEN
101
Minnetonka
Lake
LRT Trail
Lynwood Ter.
Delton Ave.
7
SHOREWOOD
Vinehill
Purgatory Park
P
Scenic Heights
Match Line
Townline

At most uncontrolled intersections with major roadways, the trail crosses the road in a pedestrian underpass or overpass. The trail system is plowed during the winter months, making it available throughout the year. Cross country skiing and snowmobiling are prohibited.

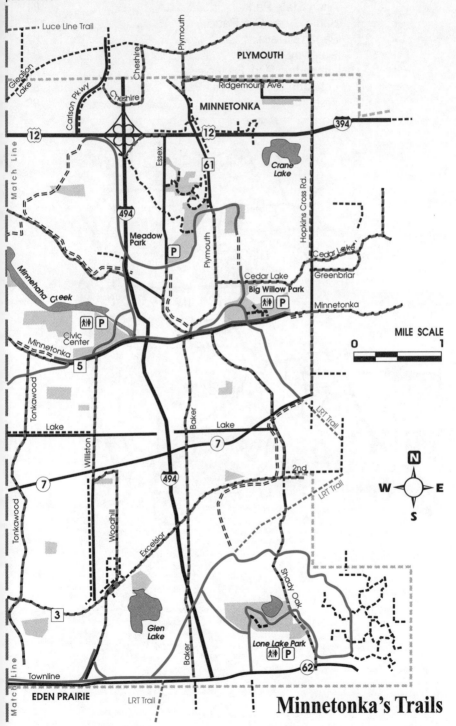

Minnetonka's Trails

East Metro

Minneapolis
St. Paul Area

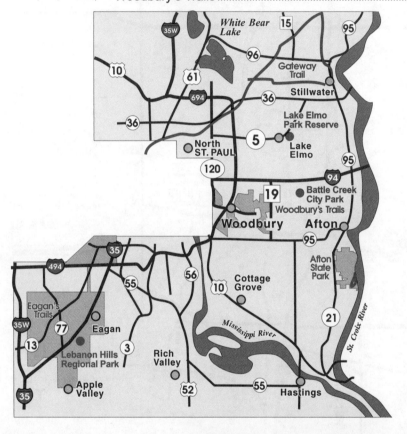

Afton State Park

Trail Length	4.0 miles
Surface	Asphalt
Uses	Leisure bicycling, cross country skiing, hiking
Location & Setting	Located less than an hour from the Twin Cities in Washington County. The park entrance is off Highway 20, just east of Highway 21. Afton State Park lies on the bluffs overlooking the St. Croix River where it is cut by deep ravines. Outcrops of sandstone jut from the side of the ravines. The rugged terrain affords spectacular view of the St. Croix Valley. Above the forested ravines are rolling fields and pastures.
Information	Afton State Park Manager (651) 436-5391
County	Washington

LEGEND

P	Parking	🎪	Picnic Area
Shelter		?	Information
Water		Restrooms	
Camping		Overlooks ■	

——— Bicycle Trail
- - - - - Alternate Use Trail
——— Roadway

Afton State Park was established in 1969. The park offer opportunities for biking, hiking, cross country skiing, swimming, picnicking and camping. Wildlife includes fox, deer, badgers, hawks, eagles and warblers. In addition to biking, there are 18.0 miles of hiking and cross country ski trails and 5 miles of horseback riding trails. The Visitor Center facilities include interpretive, information and a pay telephone. The camp is closed from 10 pm to 8 am except for campers.

To AFTON 4 mi.

Afton State Park

Trout Brook

Afton Alps Ski Area

Prairie Restoration

Backpack Camping Area

Prairie Restoration

Park Entrance

Trail Heads

Lake St. Croix

To POINT DOUGLAS 6 mi.

MILE SCALE

0   1

Eagan's Trails

Trail Length	Over 50.0 miles
Surface	Paved
Uses	Leisure bicycling, in-line skating, jogging
Location & Setting	The city of Eagan, southeast of the Twin Cities. The routes includes connections between Fort Snelling State Park, the Zoo, Lebanon Hills Regional Park and the Minnesota Valley Visitor Center. While the routes are mostly off-road, many are hilly.
Information	Fort Snelling State Park (651) 725-2390
County	Dakota

LEGEND
- P Parking
- ⓘ Refreshments
- ☂ Water
- ? Information
- MF Multi-Facilities Available
- 🚻 Restrooms

Refreshments   Lodging   Telephone
First Aid   Picnic   Restrooms

━━━━━ Bicycle Trail
          Bikeway
- - - - - Alternate Bike Trail
          Roadway

Dakota County Parks

Spring Lake Park Reserve
Hiking, cross countryskiing & scenic trails wind through woods and along the bluffs high above the Mississippi River. Park visitors will enjoy activities such as a model airplane flying field and archery trail. Facilities include: a heated lodge, an outdoor classroom and a large open playfield with a sand volleyball court. South of Twin Cities on Hwy 55 to CR 42, east 2 mi. 8am to 11pm.

Lake Byllesby Regional Park
Camping, canoeing, hiking and sailing are just a few of the activities you can enjoy at Lake Byllesby Regional Park. Nestled in the Cannon Valley along the shore of Lake Byllesby Reservoir, the park offers many acres of woods and open area and a large beautiful lake. South of Twin Cities on Hwy 52 to CR86 (near Cannon Falls). West on CR 86, immediate left on Harry Ave, south 1.5 mi. 5am to 11pm.

Lebanon Hills
Activities such as biking, camping, canoeing, hiking, nature interpretation, cross country skiing and snowshoeing are available to visitors of Lebanon Hills Regional Park, which consists of over 2,000 acres of lakes, hills and woods, and a beautiful swimming beach. See the map inset of the park for mountain biking or hiking alternatives. The mountain biking trail is hilly and located in deep hardwoods. Its surface is dirt and grass. 5am to 11pm, swim beach open 11am to 8pm.

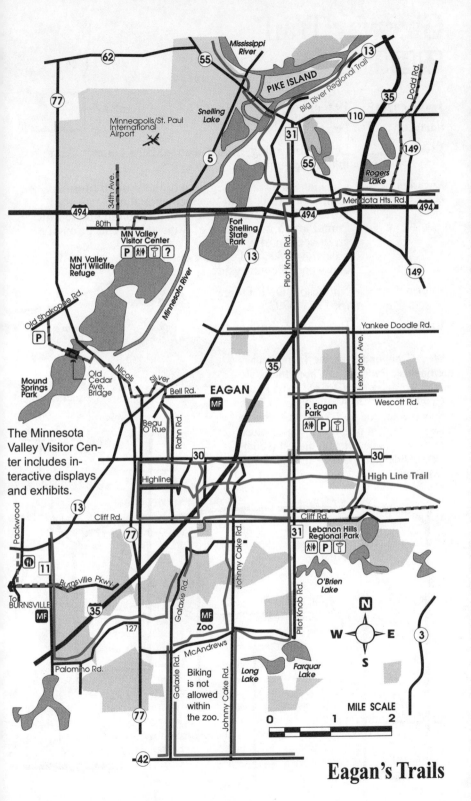

The Minnesota Valley Visitor Center includes interactive displays and exhibits.

Eagan's Trails

Gateway Trail

Trail Length	19.6 miles
Surface	Paved
Uses	Leisure bicycling, in-line skating, cross country skiing, hiking/jogging
Location & Setting	The Gateway Trail, a segment of the Willard Munger State Trail, is a paved, multi-use recreational trail starting 1 mile north of downtown St. Paul and continuing to Pine Point Park, 5 miles north of Stillwater. It cuts through a cross-section of urban area and parks, and extends out to lakes, wetlands, fields and wooded countryside.
Information	Minnesota DNR Office (651) 772-7935
Counties	Ramsey, Washington

West Trailhead Take the Larpenteur & Wheelock Parkway exit from Interstate 35E (3 miles north of downtown St. Paul). Go east 1 block to Westminister St. Turn right (south) and go 1/2 mile to Arlington Ave. Turn right (west) and go 1/2 block to the trail parking lot on the left (south) side of Arlington (near the Interstate 35E overpass).

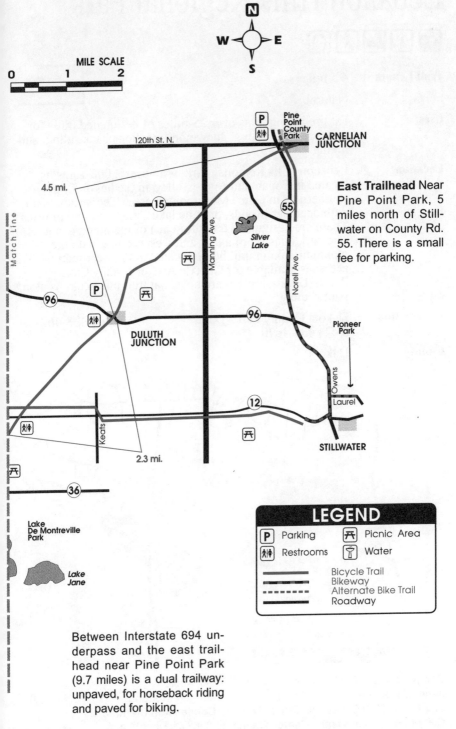

MILE SCALE
0 1 2

N
W E
S

120th St. N.

P
Pine Point County Park
CARNELIAN JUNCTION

East Trailhead Near Pine Point Park, 5 miles north of Stillwater on County Rd. 55. There is a small fee for parking.

4.5 mi.

15

55

Match Line

Silver Lake

Manning Ave.

Norell Ave.

96

P

96

DULUTH JUNCTION

Pioneer Park

Owens

Laurel

Keats

12

STILLWATER

2.3 mi.

36

Lake De Montreville Park

Lake Jane

LEGEND
P	Parking	🏕	Picnic Area
🚻	Restrooms	Water	

Bicycle Trail
Bikeway
Alternate Bike Trail
Roadway

Between Interstate 694 underpass and the east trailhead near Pine Point Park (9.7 miles) is a dual trailway: unpaved, for horseback riding and paved for biking.

Gateway Trail

Lebanon Hills Regional Park

Trail Length	4.5 miles
Surface	Natural
Uses	Fat tire biking, plus over 25-miles of designated trails for cross-country skiing, snowmobiling, horseback riding, and hiking.
Location & Setting	Lebanon Hills Regional Park, with over 2,000-acres, is located in Eagan and Apple Valley, in the heart of the southern Twin Cities Metropolitan area. The terrain is hilly with deep hardwoods, pristine lakes, marshes, and prairies. There are designated trails for each of the numerous uses. The park consists of a east and west section, with the mountain biking trail being located in the west section. Trail access is available off Galaxle Ave. or Johnny Cake Ridge Road. Location maps are posted at trail intersections along your route.
Information	Dakota County Parks Dept. (651) 438-4670 (651) 438-4671 or
County	Dakota

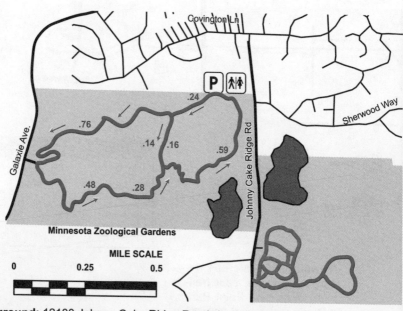

Campground: 12100 Johnny Cake Ridge Road, Apple Valley. **Jensen Trailhead:** 1350 Carriage Hills Drive, Eagan. **Holland Trailhead:** 1100 Cliff Road, Eagan. **Schulze Concession Stand:** 832 Cliff Road, Eagan. **Visitor Center/Trailhead:** 836 Cliff Road, Eagan. **Camp Sacajawea:** 5121 McAndrews Road, Apple Valley.

Sharing the Trail with Others:

* Stay on the designated trail.

* Keep right so others can pass

* Keep all pets on leash/ Properly dispose of pet waste

* Obey traffic signs and rules.

* Pack out all garbage and litter.

* Respect adjoining landowners rights and privacy.

* Warn other trail users when passing by giving an audible signal. Some horses may be spooked by quiet bikers or in-line skaters. Let them know you are passing.

* Overnight camping and campfires are permitted only on designated campsites. Do not leave campfires unattended.

* Enjoy the beauty of wild plants & animals, but leave them undisturbed for all to enjoy.

* Trail users are legally responsible for obeying the Minnesota's rules and regulations.

Woodbury's Trails

Woodbury's Trails

Trail Length	35.0+ miles
Surface	Paved

Uses	Leisure bicycling, in-line skating, hiking/jogging
Location & Setting	The city of Woodbury is located southeast of the Twin Cities. The route forms a large loop through the city. A good place to start is Ojibway Park. Exit I-494 on Valley Creek Road. Head east to Woodlane Drive and then south to Courtly Road. East on Courtly Road to Ojibway Drive and then south on Ojibway Drive for one block to the park entrance.
Information	Woodbury Parks & Recreation Department (651) 739-5972
County	Washington

LEGEND

🚰 Water	🚻 Restrooms

Bicycle Trail
Bikeway
Alternate Bike Trail
Roadway

MILE SCALE

0   1

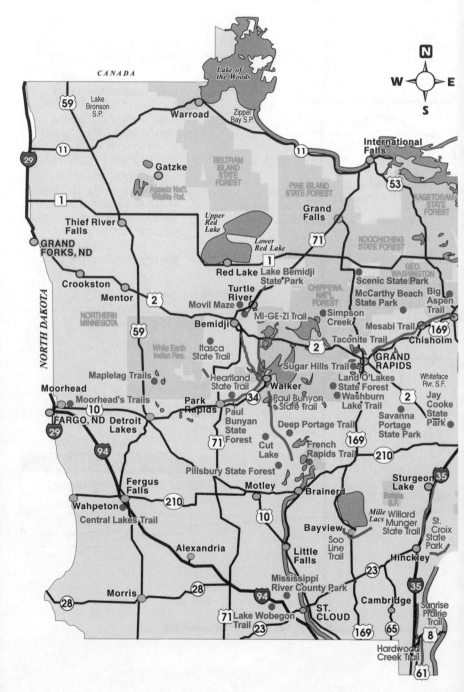

CANADA

Lake of
the Woods

Lake
Bronson
S.P.

Zippel
Bay S.P.

Warroad

Gatzke

BELTRAMI
ISLAND
STATE
FOREST

PINE ISLAND
STATE FOREST

International
Falls

Agassiz Nat'l.
Wildlife Ref.

Upper
Red
Lake

Grand
Falls

KOOCHICHING
STATE FOREST

KAGETOGAMA
STATE
FOREST

Thief River
Falls

Lower
Red Lake

GEO.
WASHINGTON
STATE FOREST

GRAND
FORKS, ND

Red Lake

Lake Bemidji
State Park

Scenic State Park

McCarthy Beach
State Park

Big
Aspen
Trail

Crookston

Turtle
River

CHIPPEWA
NAT'L.
FOREST

Mentor

Movil Maze

Simpson
Creek

Mesabi Trail

MI-GE-ZI Trail

Chisholm

NORTHERN
MINNESOTA

Bemidji

Taconite Trail

White Earth
Indian Res.

Itasca
State Trail

Sugar Hills Trail

GRAND
RAPIDS

Maplelag Trails

Heartland
State Trail

Walker

Land O'Lakes
State Forest

Whiteface
Rvr. S.F.

Moorhead

Moorhead's Trails

Park
Rapids

Paul Bunyan
State Trail

Washburn
Lake Trail

Jay
Cooke
State
Park

FARGO, ND

Detroit
Lakes

Paul
Bunyan
State
Forest

Deep Portage Trail

Savanna
Portage
State Park

Cut
Lake

French
Rapids Trail

Fergus
Falls

Pillsbury State Forest

Motley

Brainerd

Sturgeon
Lake

Wahpeton

Central Lakes Trail

Solana
S.F.

Mille
Lacs

Willard
Munger
State Trail

St.
Croix
State
Park

Alexandria

Bayview

Little
Falls

Soo
Line
Trail

Hinckley

Morris

Mississippi
River County Park

Cambridge

Sunrise
Prairie
Trail

Lake Wobegon
Trail

ST.
CLOUD

Hardwood
Creek Trail

N
W E
S

Northern Minnesota

Grand Portage

Cascade Trail

Pincushion Mountain

169

Hidden Valley/Trezona Trail

Pancore Trail

Whitefish Lake

Grand Marais

Eliason Tower Trail

Timber/Frear Trail

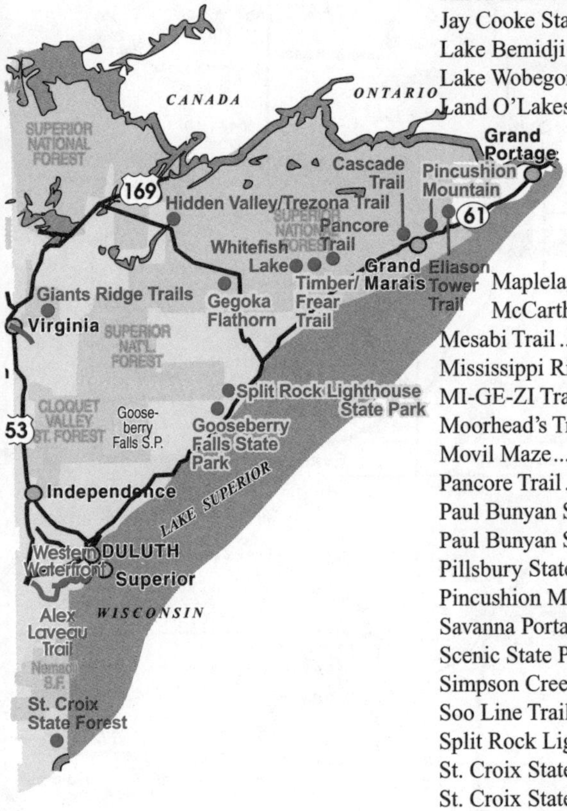

CANADA

ONTARIO

SUPERIOR NATIONAL FOREST

SUPERIOR NAT'L FOREST

61

Giants Ridge Trails

Gegoka Flathorn

Virginia

SUPERIOR NAT'L FOREST

Split Rock Lighthouse State Park

CLOQUET VALLEY ST. FOREST

53

Gooseberry Falls S.P.

Gooseberry Falls State Park

Independence

LAKE SUPERIOR

Western Waterfront

DULUTH

Superior

Alex Laveau Trail

WISCONSIN

Nemadji S.F.

St. Croix State Forest

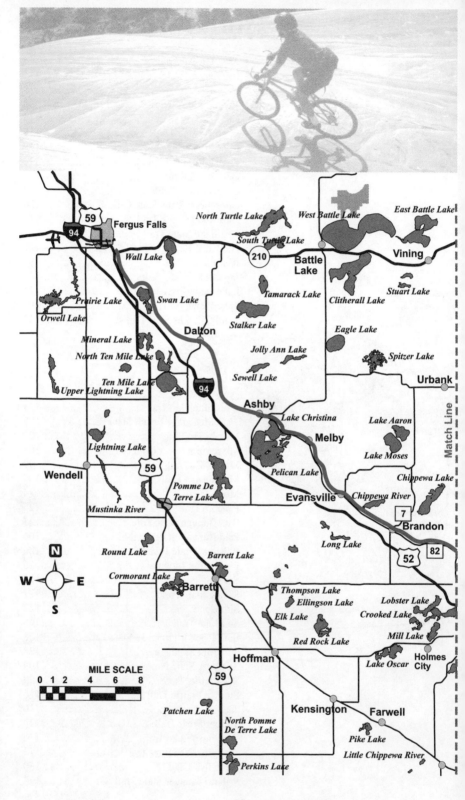

Central Lakes Trail

Trail Length	69 miles
Surface	Asphalt, gravel
Uses	Both leisure & fat tire bicycling, hiking, cross-country skiing
Location & Setting	This 69 mile trail was developed on old railbed and runs between Fergus Falls and Osakis, with a planned extension to Sauk Centre. The 18 mile stretch between Osakis and Garfield is asphalt; the 16 miles between Garfield and the Douglas County line is gravel, and the remaining 21 miles to Fergis Falls is asphalt. The setting is rural with several communities in route.
Information	Central Lakes Trail Office (320) 763-6001
Counties	Douglas, Grant, Otter Tail, Stearns, Todd

MILE SCALE
0 1 2   4   6   8

Parkers Prairie
Lake Adley
Eagle Bend
71
Clarissa
Match Line
Rose City
Lake Miltona
Miltona
71
Lake Carlos
Lake Ida
Carlos
N
W—E
S
Long Prairie
29
71
Garfield
Darling Lake
Lake Le Homme Dieu
Lake Osakis
Round Prairie
Lake Minn
Alexandria
27
Little Sauk Lake
Sauk River
Little Sauk
Osakis
Smith Lake
Guernsey Lake
Andrew Lake
29
94
West Union
Ward Springs
Little Birch Lake
Lake Mary
Forada
Maple Lake
Sauk Lake
Lake Reno
Leven Lake
Westport
Sauk Centre
Villard Lake
Wesport Lake
71

93

Heartland State Trail

Trail Length	50.0 miles
Surface	Asphalt, natural-groomed
Uses	Leisure bicycling, cross-country skiing, in-line skating, snowmobiling, hiking
Location & Setting	The Heartland Trail is a 50 mile multiple-use state trail constructed on an abandoned railroad line. The Trail has two segments. The East-West segment is 28 miles long and asphalt paved, running between Park Rapids Walker. The North-South segment is 22 miles long, undeveloped but mowed, and runs between Walker and just south of Cass Lake. The East West segment is mostly open area while the North-South segment is wooded and lakes.
Information	Heartland Trail Headquarters (218) 652-4054
Counties	Hubbard, Cass

West Trailhead—Begins in Heartland Park in Park Rapids. Going east on HWY 34 through Park Rapids, you turn north on Central Avenue (there is a sign). Turn west on North Street which leads into the park which offers excellent facilities.

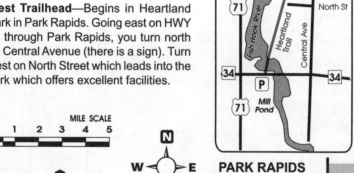

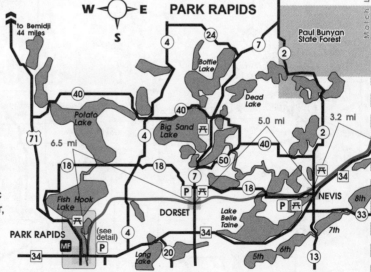

PARK RAPIDS is named for the park-like groves and prairies that existed. Parking, restrooms, water, picnic area, shelter, restaurants, and lodging available in the area.

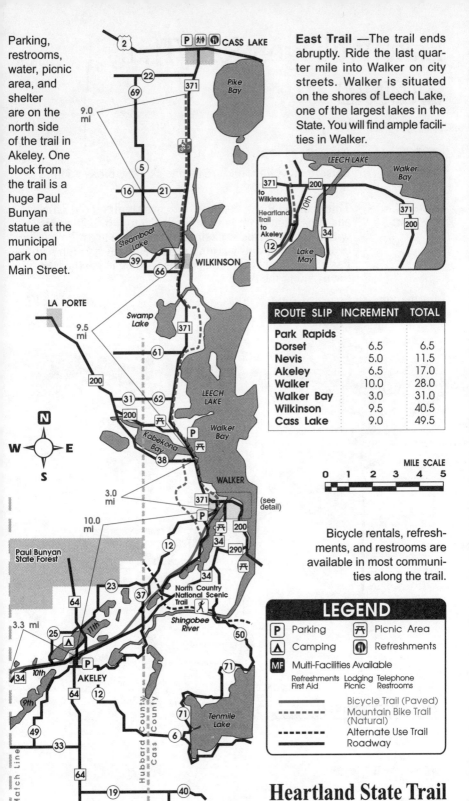

Parking, restrooms, water, picnic area, and shelter are on the north side of the trail in Akeley. One block from the trail is a huge Paul Bunyan statue at the municipal park on Main Street.

East Trail —The trail ends abruptly. Ride the last quarter mile into Walker on city streets. Walker is situated on the shores of Leech Lake, one of the largest lakes in the State. You will find ample facilities in Walker.

ROUTE SLIP	INCREMENT	TOTAL
Park Rapids		
Dorset	6.5	6.5
Nevis	5.0	11.5
Akeley	6.5	17.0
Walker	10.0	28.0
Walker Bay	3.0	31.0
Wilkinson	9.5	40.5
Cass Lake	9.0	49.5

MILE SCALE
0 1 2 3 4 5

Bicycle rentals, refreshments, and restrooms are available in most communities along the trail.

LEGEND

P	Parking	🎋	Picnic Area
A	Camping	🍴	Refreshments
MF	Multi-Facilities Available		

Refreshments Lodging Telephone
First Aid Picnic Restrooms

——— Bicycle Trail (Paved)
- - - - - Mountain Bike Trail (Natural)
– – – – Alternate Use Trail
——— Roadway

Heartland State Trail

Lake Wobegon Rail-Trail

Trail Length	28 miles
Surface	Asphalt
Uses	Leisure bicycling, hiking, in-line skating, cross-country skiing
Location & Setting	This trail, which opened in 1998, was built on old railbed and runs from Avon west to Sauk Centre. It is 28 miles long with a 10 foot wide asphalt surface. There are mile markers every half mile and warning signs before every stop sign. Parking and most facilities are accessible in each of the 5 towns along the route.
Information	Stearns County Parks (320) 255-6172
County	Stearns

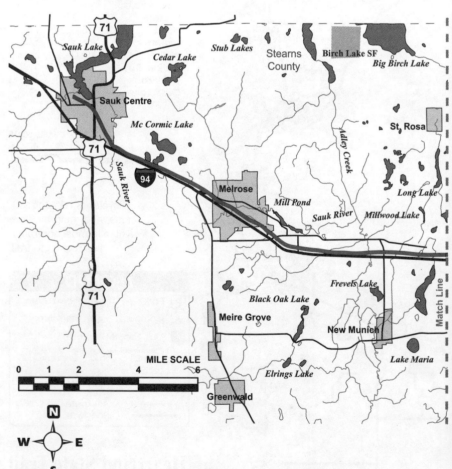

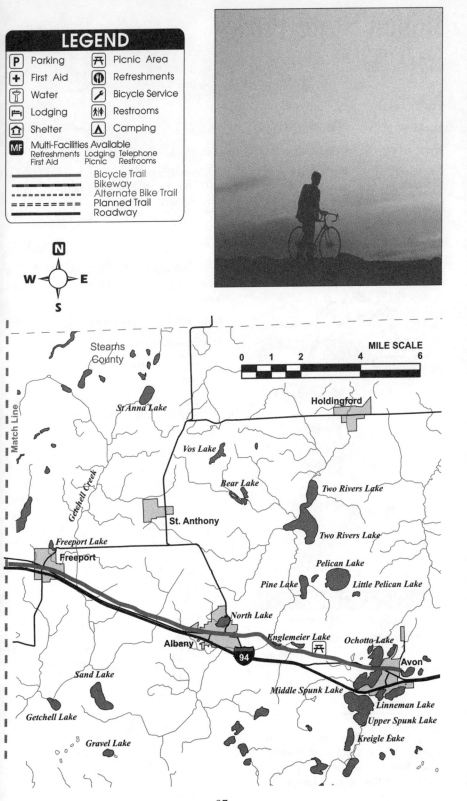

LEGEND

P	Parking	🛏 Picnic Area	
+	First Aid	🍴 Refreshments	
🚰	Water	🔧 Bicycle Service	
🛏	Lodging	🚻 Restrooms	
🏠	Shelter	🅰 Camping	

MF Multi-Facilities Available
Refreshments Lodging Telephone
First Aid Picnic Restrooms

———— Bicycle Trail
———— Bikeway
-------- Alternate Bike Trail
======== Planned Trail
Roadway

N
W — **E**
S

Match Line

Stearns County

St Anna Lake

MILE SCALE
0   1   2   4   6

Holdingford

Vos Lake

Bear Lake

Two Rivers Lake

Getchell Creek

St. Anthony

Two Rivers Lake

Freeport Lake

Freeport

Pelican Lake

Pine Lake

Little Pelican Lake

North Lake

Englemeier Lake

Ochotto Lake

Albany

94

Avon

Sand Lake

Middle Spunk Lake

Linneman Lake

Getchell Lake

Upper Spunk Lake

Gravel Lake

Kreigle Lake

Itasca State Park

Trail Length	17.0 miles
Surface	Asphalt, roadway
Uses	Leisure bicycling, cross-country skiing, in-line skating, hiking
Location & Setting	Itasca State Park, where the Mississippi River begins, is a 32,000 acre park established in 1891. It is located 20 miles north of Park Rapids, on Hwy. 71. Heavily wooded, lakes.
Information	Itasca State Park Manager (218) 266-3654
Counties	Clearwater, Hubbard, Becker

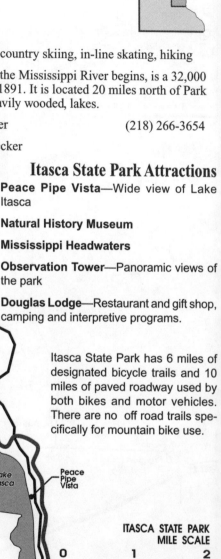

Itasca State Park Attractions

Peace Pipe Vista—Wide view of Lake Itasca

Natural History Museum

Mississippi Headwaters

Observation Tower—Panoramic views of the park

Douglas Lodge—Restaurant and gift shop, camping and interpretive programs.

Itasca State Park has 6 miles of designated bicycle trails and 10 miles of paved roadway used by both bikes and motor vehicles. There are no off road trails specifically for mountain bike use.

LEGEND

P	Parking	🌲	Picnic Area
🛏	Lodging	🅦	Refreshments
▲	Camping	?	Information
🚻	Restrooms		
———	Bicycle Trail		
———	Roadway		

ITASCA STATE PARK
MILE SCALE

0   1   2

Bicycle Rental Available during the summer at the Itasca boat landing.
Boat Tours Available during the summer by the Douglas Lodge.

Mi-GE-ZI Trail

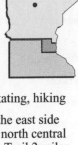

Trail Length	18 miles
Surface	Asphalt - 8 to 10 feet wide
Uses	Leisure bicycling, cross-country skiing, in-line skating, hiking
Location & Setting	The MI-GE-ZI Trail winds around Pike Bay and the east side of Cass Lake on the Chippewa National Forest in north central Minnesota. It also connects to the Heartland State Trail 2 miles south of Cass Lake. The Trail runs along glittering lakes and through towering pine forests.
Information	USDA Forest Service, Walker Ranger District (218) 547-1044
County	Hubbard

The MI-GE-ZI Trail was named in the Anishinabe language for the bald eagle.

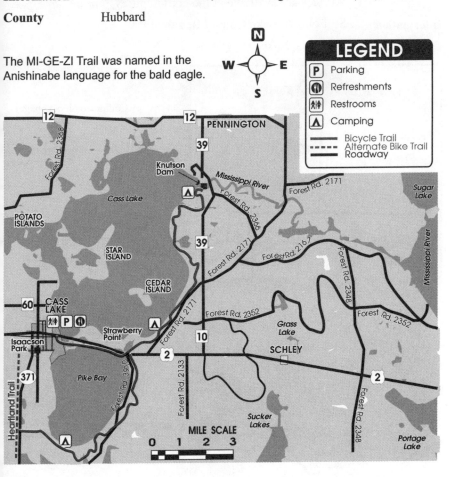

Mesabi Trail

Trail Length	66 miles
Surface	Asphalt
Uses	Leisure bicycling, hiking, in-line skating
Location & Setting	Some 66 miles of this planned 132 mile trail between Grand Rapids and Ely are completed and asphalt paved. The longest paved sections run from Grand Rapids to Taconite for 13 miles; from Nashwauk east to Kinney for 30 miles; and from Mt. Iron to Eveleth for 13 miles. The trail is partially built on old railbed and is 10 to 14 feet wide. Most services are available at the communities in route.
Information	St. Louis & Lake County Regional Rail
Counties	St. Louis, Lake

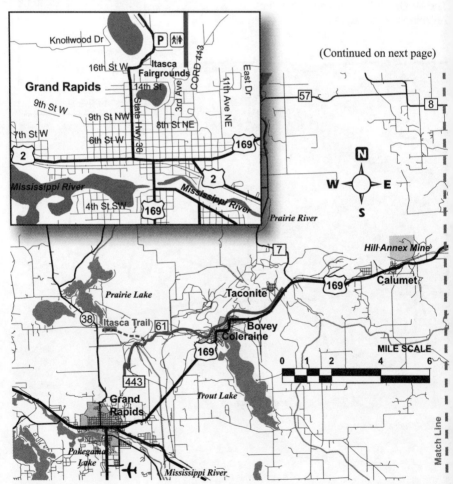

(Continued on next page)

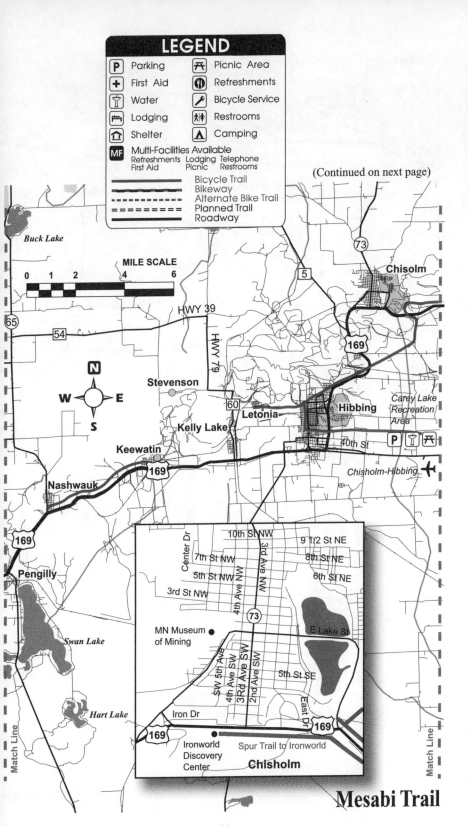

LEGEND

P	Parking	🎪	Picnic Area
+	First Aid	🍴	Refreshments
🚰	Water	🔧	Bicycle Service
🛏	Lodging	🚹🚺	Restrooms
🏠	Shelter	⛺	Camping

MF Multi-Facilities Available
Refreshments Lodging Telephone
First Aid Picnic Restrooms

—————— Bicycle Trail
Bikeway
-=-=-=-=- Alternate Bike Trail
========= Planned Trail
Roadway

(Continued on next page)

Buck Lake

MILE SCALE

0 1 2 4 6

HWY 39

65

54

HWY 73

N
W E
S

Stevenson

60

Letonia

Kelly Lake

Keewatin

169

Nashwauk

169

Pengilly

Swan Lake

Hart Lake

Match Line

5

Chisolm

73

169

Hibbing

Carey Lake
Recreation
Area

40th St

P 🚰 🎪

Chisholm-Hibbing ✈

10th St NW

Center Dr

7th St NW

5th St NW

3rd St NW

3rd Ave NW

4th Ave NW

73

9 1/2 St NE

8th St NE

6th St NE

E Lake St

MN Museum
of Mining

SW 5th Ave SW

4th Ave SW

3Rd Ave SW

2nd Ave SW

5th St SE

East Dr

Iron Dr

169

Ironworld
Discovery
Center

Spur Trail to Ironworld

169

Chisholm

Match Line

Mesabi Trail

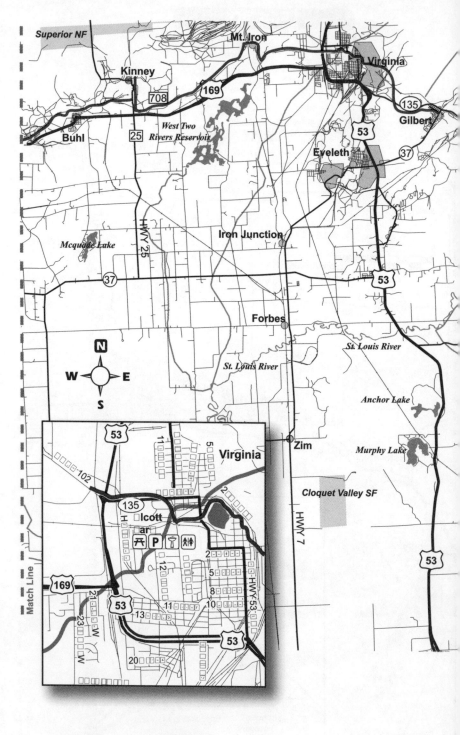

Superior NF

Mt. Iron

Virginia

Kinney

708   169

135

Gilbert

Buhl

25   West Two
Rivers Reservoir

53

37

Eveleth

HWY 25

Mcquade Lake

Iron Junction

37   53

Forbes

N
W   E
S

St. Louis River

St. Louis River

Anchor Lake

Zim

Murphy Lake

Cloquet Valley SF

53

HWY 7

Match Line

Virginia (inset)

53

102

135   lcott

ar

冹 P Ŧ 朴

169

21

23

53

13

11

12

2

5

8

10

5

2

HWY 53

53

20

53

Mesabi Trail

Mississippi River County Park

Trail Length	2.5 miles
Surface	Crushed stone
Uses	Leisure bicycling, hiking, cross-country skiing
Location & Setting	This County Park has 2.5 miles of year round trails. It's located about 6 miles north of Sartell and 10 miles north of St. Cloud. The setting is woods, prairies and open area. Facilities include toilets, shelters, picnic areas and a boat launch.
Information	Stearns County Parks (320) 255-6172
Counties	Stearns

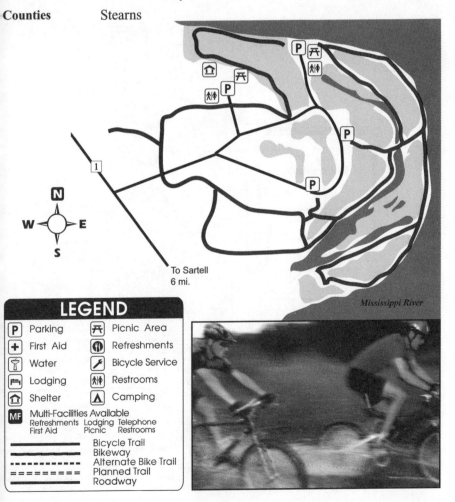

To Sartell
6 mi.

Mississippi River

LEGEND

P	Parking	🎪	Picnic Area
✚	First Aid	🍷	Refreshments
🚰	Water	🔧	Bicycle Service
🛏	Lodging	🚻	Restrooms
🏠	Shelter	⛺	Camping
MF	Multi-Facilities Available		

Refreshments Lodging Telephone
First Aid Picnic Restrooms

—————— Bicycle Trail
            Bikeway
------------ Alternate Bike Trail
========= Planned Trail
━━━━━━ Roadway

Moorhead's Trails

Trail Length	12.5 miles
Surface	Paved
Uses	Leisure bicycling, hiking, in-line skating, cross-country skiing
Location & Setting	Much of the trail parallels 11th St. and Hwy 20 in Moorhead. Other off-road trails include a 25 mile trail paralleling the Red River across from Moorhead in North Dakota, and a trail east of Moorhead in Dilworth along Hwy 10.
Information	Moorhead Parks Dept. (218) 299-5340
County	Clay

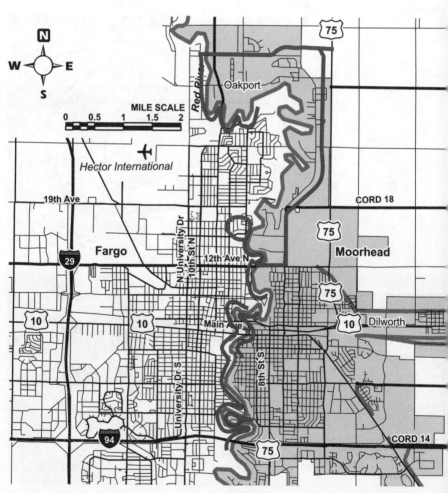

Explanation of Symbols

ROUTES

━━━━━ Biking Trail
▬▬▬▬ Bikeway
▬ ▬ ▬ ▬ Alternate Bike Trail
▪▪▪▪▪ Undeveloped Trail
▪ ▪ ▪ ▪ Alternate Use Trail
= = = = Planned Trail
━━━━━ Roadway

TRAIL USES

 Mountain Biking

 Leisure Biking

 In Line Skating

 (X-C) Cross-Country Skiing

 Hiking

Horseback Riding

 Snowmobiling

FACILITIES

🔧 Bike Repair

⛺ Camping

➕ First Aid

❓ Info

🛏 Lodging

🅿 Parking

🔲 Picnic

🍴 Refreshments

🚻 Restrooms

🏠 Shelter

⛲ Water

MF Multi Facilities

Refreshments   First Aid
Telephone   Picnic
Restrooms   Lodging

ROAD RELATED SYMBOLS

 Interstate Highway

🛡45 U.S. Highway

45 State Highway

45 County Highway

AREA DESCRIPTIONS

 Parks, Schools, Preserves, etc.

 Waterway

 Mileage Scale

Directional

Paul Bunyon State Trail

Trail Length	100 miles
Surface	see chart below
Uses	Leisure bicycling, cross-country skiing, in-line skating, snowmobiling, hiking
Location & Setting	North central Minnesota. Primarily located on abandoned rail grade, the trail links the towns of Brainerd, Walker and Bemidji plus several other small communities in route. It is generally level. Woods, lakes & open country.
Information	Minnesota Department of Natural Resources (218) 755-2265
Counties	Crow Wing, Cass, Hubbard, Beltrami

FROM	SURFACE	WIDTH	LENGTH	MAP SYMBOL
Brainerd/Baxter to Hackensack	asphalt	10 ft wide	48.5 miles	A
Lake Bemidji to Mississippi River	asphalt	12 ft wide	5.3 miles	A
Walker to Hubard/Beltrami County line	ballast*	10 ft wide	28.0 miles	B
Hubbard/Betrami County line to Bemidji	ballast*	10 ft wide	18.0 miles	B

* asphalt planned

Mileage Guide

	INCREMENT	TOTALS
Baxter		100.0
Merrifield	9.0	9.0 ... 91.0
Nisswa	5.8	14.8 ... 85.2
Pequot Lakes	6.2	21.0 ... 79.0
Jenkins	3.0	24.0 ... 76.0
Pine River	6.0	30.0 ... 70.0
Backus	8.8	38.8 ... 61.2
Elackensack	7.6	46.4 ... 53.6
Walker	16.8	63.2 ... 36.8
Benedict	7.8	71.0 ... 29.0
Laporte	5.2	76.2 ... 23.8
Guthrie	6.2	82.4 ... 17.6
Nary	5.2	87.6 ... 12.4
Bemidji	9.6	97.2 ... 2.8
Lake Bemidji SP	2.8	100.0

Crow Wing State Park

Phone: (218) 829-8022

The historic Red River Ox Cart Trail goes through the once prosperous town of Old Crow Wing. Park visitors will enjoy the natural beauty of the confluence of the Crow Wing and Mississippi Rivers. Hike the 18 mi of trails to capture a sense of the area's history. 6.4 mi of cross-country ski. Year round. 8am-10pm daily. Parking permit fee. Located 9 mi S of Brainerd on Hwy 371. Park headquarters 1 mi west of 371 on Co Rd 27.

Parking Available in Baxter, Merrifield, Nisswa, Pequot Lakes, Jenkins, Pine River, Backus, Hackensack and Walker.

The south trailhead is located in Baxter. From Brainerd, go west on Highway 210 about 3/4 of a mile. Turn north (right) on Highway 371 to the first stoplight (Excelsior Road). Turn east (right), and continue to the parking lot.

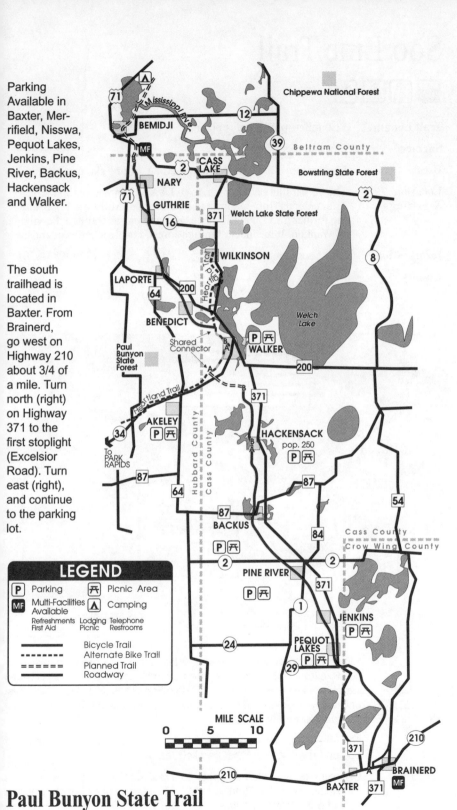

Chippewa National Forest

BEMIDJI

Beltram County

CASS LAKE

Bowstring State Forest

NARY

GUTHRIE

Welch Lake State Forest

WILKINSON

LAPORTE

BENEDICT

Paul Bunyon State Forest

Shared Connector

Welch Lake

WALKER

Heartland Trail

AKELEY

To PARK RAPIDS

HACKENSACK
pop. 250

BACKUS

Hubbard County
Cass County

PINE RIVER

Cass County
Crow Wing County

JENKINS

PEQUOT LAKES

BRAINERD

BAXTER

LEGEND

P	Parking	🌲	Picnic Area
MF	Multi-Facilities Available	🏕	Camping
	Refreshments First Aid	Lodging Picnic	Telephone Restrooms

——— Bicycle Trail
- - - - - Alternate Bike Trail
====== Planned Trail
——— Roadway

MILE SCALE

0   5   10

Paul Bunyon State Trail

Soo Line Trail

Trail Length	11.0 miles, plus 8 miles planned
Surface	Paved, 8 feet wide
Uses	Leisure bicycling, cross-country skiing, in-line skating, hiking
Location & Setting	The 10 parallel path is open to A.T.V.'s and snowmobiling. The Trail extends from Onomia to Isle, south of Mill Lacs Lake, along the former Soo Line railroad grade, and passes through the village of Wahkon. It meanders through forest, farmland and wetlands.
Information	Mill Lacs County (320) 983-8201
County	Mill Lacs

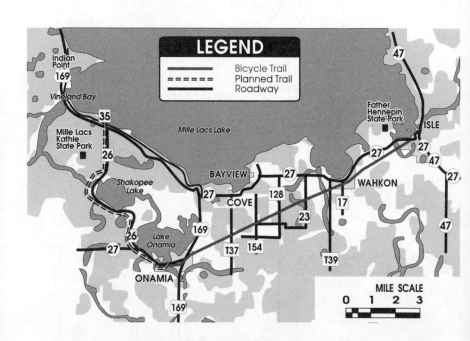

Father Hennepin State Park and Kathio State Park are both easily accessible from both ends of the trail. Father Hennepin State Park is linked via low volume city street in Isle. Kathio State Park, five miles north west of Onamia, is linked via County State Aid Highway 26 which also has a relatively low traffic volume.

The bike trail is within a duel use corridor. There is also a ten foot unpaved portion for A.T.V. users that parallels the bike trail.

Onamia has renovated a depot into a rest stop along the trail. There is an exhibit, the 'Ellen Ruth" a former Mille Lacs Lake Launch, which is only one block from the trail.

St. Croix State Park

Trail Length	6.0 miles
Surface	Paved
Uses	Leisure bicycling, cross-country skiing, in-line skating, hiking
Location & Setting	St. Croix State Park borders the St. Croix River and Wisconsin state line and is located approximately 60 miles north of the Twin Cities and 15 miles east of Hinckley. It is the largest state park in Minnesota with over 33,000 acres of forest, meadows and streams.
Information	St. Croix State Park (320) 384-6591
County	Pine

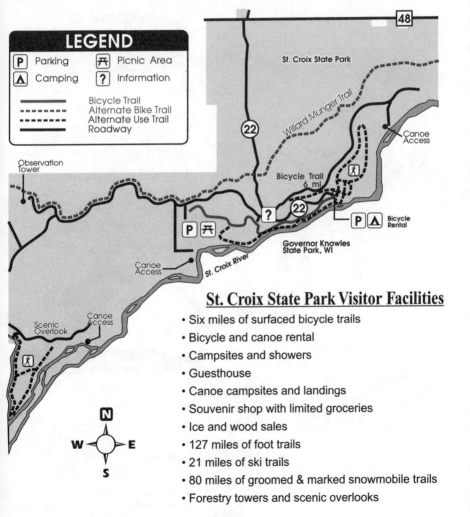

St. Croix State Park Visitor Facilities

- Six miles of surfaced bicycle trails
- Bicycle and canoe rental
- Campsites and showers
- Guesthouse
- Canoe campsites and landings
- Souvenir shop with limited groceries
- Ice and wood sales
- 127 miles of foot trails
- 21 miles of ski trails
- 80 miles of groomed & marked snowmobile trails
- Forestry towers and scenic overlooks

Taconite Trail

Trail Length	165 miles (6 miles paved)
Surface	Paved, undeveloped
Uses	Leisure bicycling, hiking, in-line skating, cross-country skiing
Location & Setting	A 165-mile trail located between Grand Rapids and Ely, of which the first 6-miles out of Grand Rapids is paved. The remaining surface is undeveloped, and is used primarily for snowmobiling.
Information	Dept. of Natural Resources Information Ctr.(651) 296-6157
Counties	St. Louis, Itasca

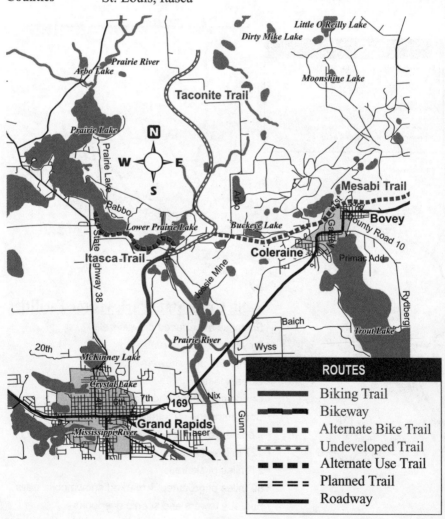

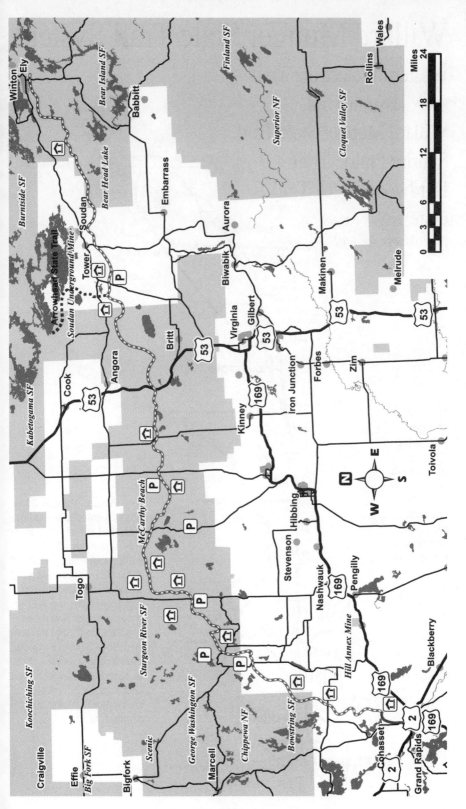

Willard Munger State Trail System

Western Waterfront Trail
Alex Laveau Trail
Willard Munger State Trail
Sunrise Prairie Trail
Hardwood Creek Trail
Gateway Trail
(East Metro Section)

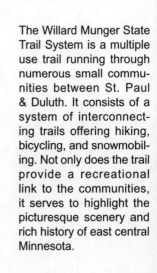

The Willard Munger Trail is the longest paved trails in the country and the greatest recreation resource in the state of Minnesota.

The Willard Munger State Trail System is a multiple use trail running through numerous small communities between St. Paul & Duluth. It consists of a system of interconnecting trails offering hiking, bicycling, and snowmobiling. Not only does the trail provide a recreational link to the communities, it serves to highlight the picturesque scenery and rich history of east central Minnesota.

Western Waterfront Trail 🚲🚶

Trail Length	5.0 miles
Surface	Paved for about a mile; rest is screenings
Uses	Leisure bicycling, hiking
Location & Setting	Located south of Duluth proper, bordering the west side of Spirit Lake and the St. Louis River. It connects to the Willard Munger Trail at its north trailhead and Commonwealth Avenue at its south trailhead.
Information	Duluth Parks & Recreation Department (218) 723-3612
Counties	Carlton

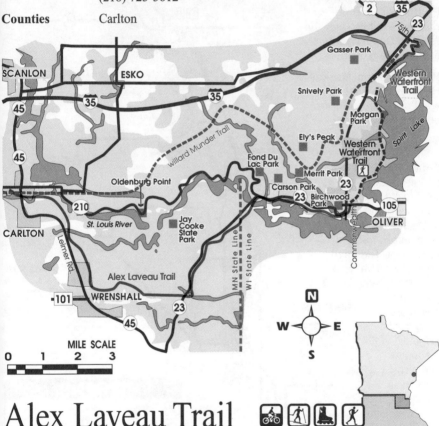

Alex Laveau Trail 🚲🎿🛼🚶

Trail Length	16 miles, including 10 miles of designated shoulder
Surface	Asphalt: 6 miles plus paved shoulder
Uses	Leisure bicycling, cross-country skiing, in-line skating, hiking
Location & Setting	From Carlton southeast through Wrenshall to Hwy. 23. North on Hwy. 23, along a designated shoulder to Hwy. 105 south of Duluth.
Information	Munger Trail Towns Association (888) 2635-0586
Counties	Carlton, St. Louis

Duluth Area Attractions

Lakewalk A mile plus boardwalk and bicycle trail from Canal Park to 26th Avenue E. along the lake shore.

Fitger's Brewery Complex Shops and restaurants along the lake shore with bike and carriage paths.

The Depot 506 W. Michigan St. • Houses 3 museums, visual arts, and 4 performing groups.

Marine Museum and Canal Park Visitor Center Interpretive geologic and maritime exhibits.

Hinckley Area Attractions

Hinckley Fire Museum Features logging and railroad exhibits, and the restored Depot Agent's office and living quarters.

Hinckley Flea Market Highway 48 East, Midwest's largest indoor/outdoor Flea Market.

South Trailhead Exit I-35 at Hinckley and go west to old Highway 61. Turn north and continue to County Rd. 18; turn west across tracks to parking lot. The trailhead is within a block of a Dairy Queen and a gas station. There are restaurants, lodging, restrooms and picnic facilities in the area.

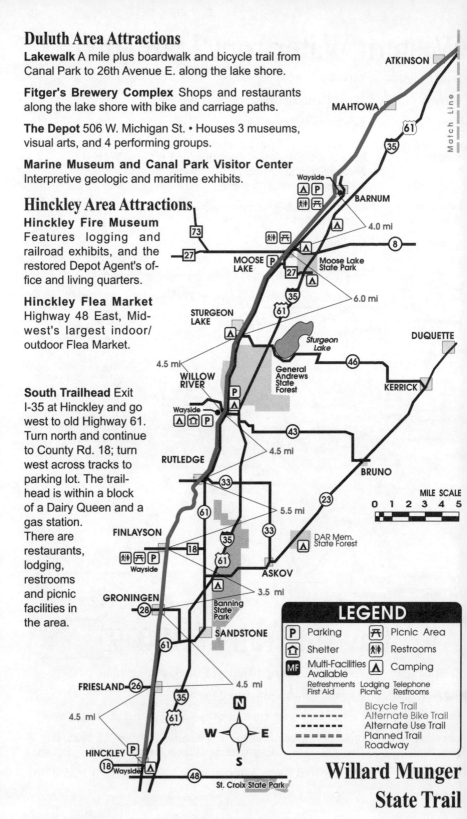

ATKINSON

MAHTOWA

Match Line

BARNUM

Wayside

4.0 mi

MOOSE LAKE

Moose Lake State Park

6.0 mi

STURGEON LAKE

Sturgeon Lake

General Andrews State Forest

DUQUETTE

KERRICK

4.5 mi

WILLOW RIVER

Wayside

RUTLEDGE

4.5 mi

BRUNO

MILE SCALE
0 1 2 3 4 5

FINLAYSON

Wayside

5.5 mi

DAR Mem. State Forest

ASKOV

3.5 mi

GRONINGEN

Banning State Park

SANDSTONE

FRIESLAND

4.5 mi

N
W E
S

4.5 mi

HINCKLEY

Wayside

St. Croix State Park

LEGEND

P	Parking	🛆	Picnic Area
⌂	Shelter	🚻	Restrooms
MF	Multi-Facilities Available	A	Camping

Refreshments First Aid   Lodging Picnic   Telephone Restrooms

Bicycle Trail
Alternate Bike Trail
Alternate Use Trail
Planned Trail
Roadway

Willard Munger State Trail

114

Willard Munger State Trail

Trail Length	76.0 miles (including 3 planned miles)
Surface	Asphalt
Uses	Leisure bicycling, cross-country skiing, in-line skating, snowmobiling, hiking
Location & Setting	The trail currently extends from Hinckley to Duluth, but will eventually run all the way from St. Paul to Duluth through a series of interconnecting trails. The trail is laid on an old railbed, asphalt surface, and largely flat with scattered forest, trees, and considerable farmland. The sections from Carlton to Duluth provides views of the St. Louis River, forest area, and rock cuts.
Information	Munger Trail Town Association (888) 263-0586
Counties	Pine, Carlton

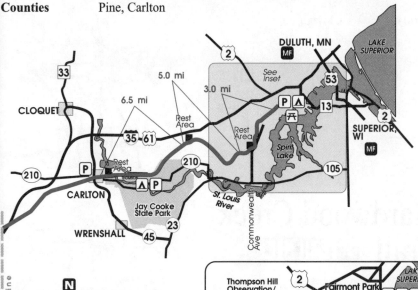

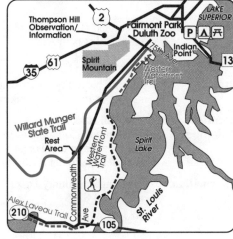

North Trailhead—On Grand Ave., Highway 23, across from the zoo at 75th Avenue. Parking, picnic area with restaurants and lodging nearby. There is a municipal campground at Indian Point within a quarter mile of the trail and on the St. Louis River.

Sunrise Prairie Trail

Trail Length	15.0 miles: 10 feet wide plus parallel dirt path
Surface	Paved
Uses	Leisure bicycling, cross-country skiing, in-line skating, hiking
Location & Setting	The trail is located in Chisago County and runs from just north of Forest Lake to North Branch. It continues parallel to Highway 61.
Information	Chisago County Parks Dept. (651) 674-2345
County	Chisago

Hardwood Creek Trail

Hardwood Creek Trail

Trail Length	9.6 miles: 10 feet wide plus parallel dirt path
Surface	Paved
Uses	Leisure bicycling, cross-country skiing, in-line skating, hiking
Location & Setting	The trail is located in Washington County and runs between Hugo and Forest Lake. It closely parallels Highway 61.
Information	Washington County Parks (651) 430-8368
County	Washington

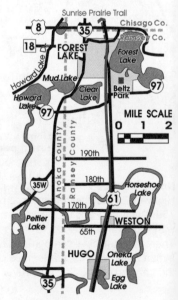

Sunrise Prairie Trail

Mountain Bicycling Opportunities

Battle Creek City Park 🚵 🚲 🚶 ⛷️

Trail Length: 7 miles

Surface: Natural

Location & Setting: Here you'll find varied terrain with single-track sections that branch off ski-trails requiring skill and climbing prowess. Effort level is moderate. Winds through open fields and hardwood forests. From south St. Paul, north on I-494, exiting on Valley Creek Rd eastbound. Continue for a half mile to Winthrop Street. Parking on left side of the street.

County: Ramsey

Big Aspen Trail 🚲 🚶 ⛷️

Trail Length: 8.5 miles

Surface: Hardpack dirt & Grass

Location & Setting: Big Aspen is located in the Superior NF. An 8.5 mile encompassing loop with many smaller loops. The setting is a large treadway that passes through forest on logging roads and old railroad grades. There are several scenic vistas, making this trail especially popular. From Virginia, take Hwy 53 north for 8 miles to CR302, then north for 1 mile to CR405. North on 405 for 2 miles to the parking lot.

County: St. Louis

Bronk Unit (R. Dorer SF) 🚲 ⛷️ 🚶 🎿

Trail Length: 7.5 miles

Surface: Packed dirt

Location & Setting: The trail consists of two narrow loops, which follow the edge of the woods as they go around the ridge. Off the north loop are spur trails, which go to the scenic overlooks of the Stockton and Mississippi River Valleys. From Stockton, north 2.1 miles to Hillsdale Township Rd. #6, then east 1.2 to the upper parking lot. Trailhead is around gate to the right.

County: Winona

Mountain Bicycling Opportunities (Continued)

Cascade Trail

Trail Length: 13 miles

Surface: Harkpack ski trail, paved & gravel road

Location & Setting: Ride starts out flat, then becomes a long climb with an elevation variance of 850 feet. There are some swampy sections, and insects can be a problem. From Tofte, northeast 16.5 miles into the Cascade Falls parking area on US 61.

County: Cook

Cut Lake

Trail Length: 10 miles

Surface: Logging roads, old ski trails

Location & Setting: Effort level is easy to moderate. Located in the Foothills SF. The trails are marked for mountain biking and there is a map at the trailhead. From Pine River, west on CR 2 for 11 miles. Entrance is on the north side.

County: Cass

Deep Portage Trail

Trail Length: 11 miles

Surface: Natural, mowed

Location & Setting: The setting is wooded and rolling. The effort level ranges from easy to difficult. Take CR 5 east of Hackensack to Woodrow Twp Rd, south to Rte 46, then east to the entrance. Parking and trailhead is by the Interpretive Center at the end of the service road.

County: Cass

Eliason Tower Trail

Trail Length: 10 miles

Surface: Gravel & grassy logging roads

Location & Setting: The west leg of the trail is a steep, 300-foot climb or descent. The east and north legs are easy and gently rolling. The south leg involves some stream crossings. Some great views of Lake Superior. No facilities along the route. From Grand Marais, northeast on Hwy 61 for 8 miles to CR 14, then north for 3 miles to the pull-off where the road makes a sharp turn to the east and you can park.

County: Cook

French Rapids Trail

Trail Length: 7.5 miles

Surface: Grass & dirt

Location & Setting: The terrain around this trail is hilly and wooded. There are sandy sections and steep climbs. The trail is not well marked. Effort level is moderate to difficult. From Brainerd northeast on Hwy 210 to airport exit (Rte 142), then left for 2.4 miles to an unmarked road. Turn left and follow to the dead end, which is the trailhead.

County: Crow Wing

Gegoka Flathorn

Trail Length: 25 miles

Surface: Natural

Location & Setting: Gegoka Flathorn is located in the Superior NF. Large loops with several optional trails. The setting consists of woods, wetlands, lakes, ponds, with rolling forest roads and some rocky hills. Forests are largely pine, birch aspen, and maple. From Isabella, Hwy 1 west about 6 miles to Gegoka Beach Lodge. Isabella is 60 miles north of Duluth on Hwy 1.

County: Lake

Mountain Bicycling Opportunities (Continued)

Giants Ridge Trail 🚴 🎿 🛷 🚶

Trail Length:	21.5 miles
Surface:	Ski Trails
Location & Setting:	Consists of 3 trails: Laurentian - 5.5 miles, easy to moderate; Silver, 6 miles, moderate to difficult; Wynne Lake Overlook - 10 miles, moderate. Well maintained ski trails. Setting varies from rolling terrain, woods to lake areas. From Biwabik east on Hwy 135 to CR 138, then north 3 miles to the entrance.
County:	St. Louis

Gooseberry Falls State Park 🚴 🎿 🛷 🚶

Trail Length:	12 miles
Surface:	Grassy singletrack
Location & Setting:	The setting for this state park includes forest, the Lake Superior shoreline, five waterfalls, and the Gooseberry River. There are many interconnecting loops. Wildlife is common. From Two Harbors, 13 miles northeast on Hwy 61, or about 35 miles north of Duluth.
County:	Lake

Hidden Valley/Trezona Trail 🚴 🎿 🚶

Trail Length:	13 miles
Surface:	Gravel roads, grassy ski trail
Location & Setting:	Effort level is moderate. Multiple loops, some steep descents, and scenic views. From Ely, Central Ave north for 2 blocks. Use parking lot behind the Wilderness Outfitters store.
County:	St. Louis

Holzinger Lodge Trail 🚵 🚶

MMM   HHH

Trail Length: 5 miles

Surface: Grass, hardpack, roots

Location & Setting: The lower 2.5 mile loop of this trail is an 8-foot wide ski trail with a moderate effort level. The upper 2.5 mile loop is challenging and single track with a 380-foot elevation gain. All services are available in Winona. From Winona, exit Hwy 14/61 at Huff St. southbound. Right on Lake Blvd. for .7 miles, then west to Holzinger Lodge.

County: Winona

Jay Cooke State Park 🚵 🚵 🚶

Trail Length: 12 miles

Surface: Grass, rocks, paved

Location & Setting: Jay Cooke State Park consists of massive rock formations, hardwoods forests, steep valleys, with beautiful views of the St. Louis River. The park offers picnic area, camping, and shelter. Trails are well maintained. Effort level is moderate. From Duluth, west on I-35W to Hwy 210, then east for 5 miles to park entrance.

County: Carlton

Kruger Unit (R. Dover SF) 🚵 🎿 🚶

Trail Length: 8.5 miles

Surface: Natural

Location & Setting: Trail is mostly double-track and rugged, over bluffs and traversing the valley of the Zumbro River. Difficulty is moderate to difficult. Located in the R. Dorer SF. From Wabasha, west on Hwy 60 to CR 81, then south for 2.5 miles past the campground to the small dirt road past the ranger station.

County: Wabasha

Lake Bemidji State Park

Trail Length: 9 miles

Surface: Grassy

Location & Setting: Surface is rolling topography with swamps and bogs, pine-moraine. Located on the north shore of Lake Bemidji, the forest is a mixture of state pine, jack pine barrens, birch, tamarack-spruce, oaks, basswood, and hard maple. From Bemidji 5 miles north and 1.7 miles east on CR 21 to park entrance.

County: Crow Wing

Lake Elmo Park Reserve

Trail Length: 8 miles

Surface: Grassy doubletrack, hardpack singletrack

Location & Setting: Effort level is easy to moderate. Rolling terrain. From I-94, north on Keats Avenue for a mile to the entrance. Parking is a ¼ mile further on the left.

County: Ramsey

Land O'Lakes State Forest

Trail Length: 15 miles

Surface: Mowed grass, dirt

Location & Setting: The setting is rolling hills, forest, lakes, and small ponds. There are numerous resorts, cabins, and private campgrounds in the forest boundary. From Outing, north on Hwy 6 to CR 48, then west 1 mile to the trailhead.

County: Cass

Lawrence Unit 🚲 🚶
(part of MN Valley State RA)

Trail Length: 13.5 miles

Surface: Grass, dirt

Location & Setting: Setting consists of wetlands, wooded areas, prairie, and savanna uplands. There are several plank bridges over marshy areas. Abundant wildlife. There is an entrance fee.

County: Scott

Maplelag Trails 🚲 🎿 🚶

Trail Length: 6.5 miles

Surface: Natural

Location & Setting: Trail sets on private land and is well maintained with moderate grades. Designed for cross-county skiing. Food, and lodging are available at Maplelag. From Callaway, go a 1/2 mile north on Hwy 59 to CR 14. East for 3 miles, then north on CR 23 for 1.7 miles. East on CR 110 (Goat Ranch Rd) for 3.5 miles to the entrance on the south side of the road.

County: Becker

McCarthy Beach State Park 🚲 🎿 🏔 🚶

Trail Length: 15.5 miles

Surface: Grassy, single and double track

Location & Setting: The Park is in a deeply wooded area with rolling hills and small valleys, located between two major lakes - Sturgeon Lake and Side Lake. The trails follow the ridge tops of the park's moraines. From Hibbing north on Hwy 169 to CR 5, then north 15 miles to the park entrance.

County: St. Louis

Mount Kato Mountain Bike Park

Trail Length:	7 miles
Surface:	Natural
Location & Setting:	Trail is mostly single-track. Effort level ranges from easy to difficult. Opened in 1996, Mount Kato's main loop, beautiful and challenging, with three climbs, and mainly moderate. From Mankato, take Hwy 169 south to Hwy 66, then south on Hwy 66 for 1 mile to the Mount Kato Ski & Bike complex.
County:	Blue Earth

Movil Maze

Trail Length:	6.5 miles
Surface:	Singletrack, grassy ski trails
Location & Setting:	Effort level is moderate to difficult. It is easy to get lost in the deep forest so bring a map. The ski trails are identified with blue diamond markers. From Bemidji, northeast on Hwy 71 for 8 miles, then north on Wildwood Road for another mile.
County:	Beltrami

Murphy-Hanrehan Park Reserve

Trail Length:	6 miles
Surface:	Natural
Location & Setting:	The terrain within the park is rugged with a number of steep hills. This is a loop on hilly ski trail, and is well maintained. Grades are long and steep. The bicycle trail is open from Mid-August through October. There is a parking fee. Located near Prior Lake. From I-35W, take CR 42 (Eagan Dr) to CR 74 (Hanrehan Lake Blvd), then south to CR 75 (Murphy Lake Blvd), continuing south to the Park entrance.
County:	Scott

Myre Big Island State Park

Trail Length: 7 miles

Surface: Grassy

Location & Setting: The Park offers rolling hills, shallow lakes, and marshes. Albert Lea Lake borders the park on the east. Located 3 miles southeast of Albert Lea. Take Exit 11 off I-35 and follow signs. Hwy 90 & I-35 intersect just north of Albert Lea.

County: Freebom

Pancore Trail

Trail Length: 16.5 miles

Surface: Old roadbed, sand, grass

Location & Setting: Terrain is flat to rolling. Located in the Superior National Forest. Area is generally well signed. From Tofte at Hwy 61, north 11.5 miles on CR 2 (Sawbill Trail) to the junction of FR338.

County: St. Louis

Paul Bunyan State Forest

Trail Length: 10 miles

Surface: Dirt & forest roads

Location & Setting: The setting is forest, ponds, bogs, and some marshy areas. There are three non-connecting loop trails. These trails are not marked, and are both single and double track. Effort level is moderate to difficult. There are no designated parking facilities. Many of the forest roads are still active. From Akeley, 10 miles north on Hwy 64 to FR 2, then left to Refuge Road and Beaver Lakes Trails, one of the three loop trails.

County: Hubbard

Mountain Bicycling Opportunities (Continued)

Pillsbury State Forest

Trail Length: 27 miles

Surface: Grassy & dirt

Location & Setting: The terrain is rolling to hilly with numerous small ponds and lakes. Effort level is moderate to difficult. Stands of maple, oak, ash, and basswood cover much of the forest. The trails are marked. From Brainerd, north and then west on CR 77 for about 10 miles. Turn southwest on Pillager FR for 2 miles. Trailhead is on the West side of road.

County: Crow Wing

Pincushion Mountain

Trail Length: 15 miles

Surface: Grassy, dirt

Location & Setting: The setting consists of forest, lowlands, bluffs, and several footbridges. Trail is single-track loops. Effort level is moderate. Pincushion Mountain offers a spectacular overview of Lake Superior and the Superior NF. From Grand Marais, go 2 miles north on CR 12. Grand Marais is about 130 miles northeast of Duluth on Hwy 61.

County: Cook

Reno Unit (R. Dorer SF)

Trail Length: 13 miles

Surface: Natural, road

Location & Setting: The Reno Unit is part of the Richard Dorer SF. The trail is narrow two-track with some dirt road. Effort level is difficult. Beautiful scenic vistas, with deep valleys and steep ridges overlooking the Mississippi River. From LaCrescent, 17 miles south on Hwy 26 to Reno. Follow the gravel road for a ¼ mile to the parking area.

County: Houston

Savanna Portage State Park

Trail Length: 12 miles

Surface: Grass, dirt roads, single track.

Location & Setting: Setting is rolling hills, lakes, bogs, and woods. Effort level is easy. The Savanna Portage was a vital link between Lake Superior and the Upper Mississippi. The rolling hills and sandy soil are remnants of past glaciers. From McGregor, take CR 14/36 northeast for 17 miles to the park entrance, then follow the gravel park road north to the Historical Marker parking area.

County: Aitkin

Scenic State Park

Trail Length: 18 miles

Surface: Single & doubletrack

Location & Setting: Maintained ski & hiking trails. Effort level is easy to moderate. The Park consists of rolling terrain, flat areas, and woods, encompassing Coon and Sandwich Lakes, and parts of several other lakes. From Bigfork, take County Road 7 south and then east a total of 7 miles to the park entrance.

County: Itasca

Simpson Creek

Trail Length: 13 miles

Surface: Singletrack

Location & Setting: Effort level is moderate and seldom cycled. Gently rolling terrain through red and white pines, along marshes, and up glacial eskers. From Deer River northwest NW Hwy 46 to parking at the Cutfoot Sioux Visitor Center.

County: Itasca

Mountain Bicycling Opportunities (Continued)

Snake Creek Unit (R. Doyer SF)

Trail Length: 8 miles

Surface: Grass and hardpack

Location & Setting: Snake Creek runs through a valley and the topography is rough with slopes rising 300-feet on either side of the valley floor. Effort level is moderate. Climbs follow reasonable grades. The area is forested with oak, pine, and walnut. Trails are well maintained, but watch for fallen branches and washout ruts. From Kellogg, go 4 miles south on Hwy 61. Follow the signs. Enter the access road, but continue straight on the field road, to the Snake Creek X-C ski area.

County: Wabasha

Split Rock Lighthouse State Park

Trail Length: 8 miles

Surface: Grass & gravel

Location & Setting: The setting for this state park is the rugged Lake Superior shoreline. Trail course varies from woods, open flat country to bumpy, loose rock and steeply pitched areas. Effort level is moderate. The Split Rock Lighthouse is said to be the most photographed lighthouse in the world. There is a history center with a theatre featuring a history film of the lighthouse. Located on Hwy 61, 20 miles northeast of Two Harbors and about 45 miles from Duluth.

County: Lake

St. Croix State Forest

Trail Length: 18 miles

Surface: Gravel, dirt road, natural

Location & Setting: Here you'll find woods, and rolling to steep hills that are often sandy and rocky. Effort level is moderate. Well into the ride there is a scenic overlook of the St. Croix River at the edge of a small ridge. Located off Hwy 48, about 22 miles east of Hinckley.

County: Pine

Sugar Hills Trail

Trail Length:	12 miles
Surface:	Grassy and hardpack, logging roads
Location & Setting:	Effort level is moderate to difficult. Setting is hilly, with many peaks, valleys, and ridges. There are many miles of unmarked trails. Be prepared with map as reference. From Grand Rapids south on Hwy 169 for 7 miles to CR 17, then west for 2 miles to CR 449. Continue west for another 3 miles, following signs to the parking lot at a former downhill skiing facility.
County:	Itasca

Timber/Frear Trail

Trail Length:	19 miles
Surface:	Gravel & unmowed old logging roads.
Location & Setting:	The ride includes two gradual climbs, one about 100 feet. Terrain is generally level to gently rolling. From Tofte at Hwy 61, north on CR 2 (Sawbill Trail), then west on FS166 for 6 miles to FS346. Proceed north 5.5 miles to FS170, then right for a mile to the Four Mile Lake boat landing at the junction of FS347.
County:	St. Louis

Trout Valley Unit (R. Dorer SF)

Trail Length:	8.5 miles
Surface:	Packed dirt, rocky
Location & Setting:	Trout valley includes steep, wooded ridges and bluffs flanking the Trout Creek. The ridge tops are open agricultural land and the slopes wooded. The trail connects the valley bottom with the ridge top, providing a scenic view of the Trout, Whitewater, and Mississippi River Valley. From Winona north on Hwy 61 to the park entrance.
County:	Winona

Mountain Bicycling Opportunities (Continued)

Washburn Lake Trail 🚵 🎿 🚶

Trail Length: 13 miles

Surface: Grassy & dirt

Location & Setting: Trail consists of two loops with a connector. Difficulty is easy to moderate. Rolling hills with lakes and small ponds. From Outing, go north on Rte 6 for 2 miles, then west on CR 48 for half a mile. Look for a sign on north side of road.

County: Cass

Whitefish Lake 🚵 🎿 🏂 🚶

Trail Length: 20 miles

Surface: Rocky doubletrack

Location & Setting: Located in the Arrowhead Region of Cook County. The trail consists of a single large loop, and skirts several lakes, ponds, and marshes. Rolling terrain and wooded areas. Effort level is moderate. From Tofte, take FR343 north to FR166, then west to FR346. North on FR346 to FF170, then left (SW) to FR357. Proceed north on FR357 to the trailhead.

County: Cook

TRAIL USES	
	Mountain Biking
	Leisure Biking
	In Line Skating
	(X-C) Cross-Country Skiing
	Hiking
	Horseback Riding
	Snowmobiling

TRAIL NAME	PAGE NO.

City to Trail Index

134

POPULATION CODES:
❶ = Up to 1,000
❷ = 1,000 to 5,000
❸ = 5,000 to 10,000
❹ = 10,000 to 50,000
❺ = Over 50,000

County to Trail Index *(Continued)*

Try A Trail!

State trails offer something for everyone in every season of the year. These trails are perfect for a close-to-home workout in an outdoor setting, for a fun day trip, or for an adventurous weekend getaway exploring Minnesota's remote reaches. These trails link urban places and country spaces, and let you explore all the beauty of Minnesota at your own pace. Historic sites, parks, forests, lakes and creeks, and charming small towns are waiting for you to discover.

You can trek through Minnesota's snowy north woods on hundreds of miles of groomed snowmobile trails, or bicycle across sunlit prairies and rolling pastoral landscapes in central Minnesota. If you haven't yet enjoyed the limestone cliffs and caves, sparkling trout streams, delicate spring wildflowers, and flashy fall colors of Minnesota's southeastern blufflands, you are in for a treat!

Small towns along the trails have put out the welcome mat for visitors to their cafes, bed-and-breakfast inns, resorts, and campgrounds. Equipment rental is available in many trail towns. Special events are held on the trails year-round, such as candle-lit cross-country ski outings. Three-day bike tours for charitable causes use parts of the Willard Munger State Trail. Other trail towns sponsor marathons, bike tours, and trail festivals. Check the DNR Website, or call the Information Center for information on special events!

Mileage Chart

	CITIES	1	2	3	4	5	6	7	8	9	10	11
1	Albert Lea		319	221	246	390	56	99	331	60	161	104
2	Bemidji	319		98	153	113	274	220	142	301	158	335
3	Brainerd	221	98		114	199	177	124	140	207	60	241
4	Duluth	246	153	114		164	225	149	253	223	138	227
5	International Falls	390	113	199	164		356	289	256	362	259	391
6	Mankato	56	274	177	225	356		76	283	80	117	125
7	Minneapolis	99	220	124	149	289	76		237	83	64	119
8	Moorhead	331	142	140	253	256	283	237		328	173	364
9	Rochester	60	301	207	223	362	80	83	328		147	45
10	St. Cloud	161	158	60	138	259	117	64	173	147		181
11	Winona	104	335	241	227	391	125	119	364	35	181	

Maps & Guide Sets for the Recreational Bicyclist by

American Bike Trails

State Trail Reference Maps

Illinois Bicycle Trails Reference Map

Iowa Bicycle Trails Reference Map

Michigan Bicycle Trails Reference Map

Minnesota Bicycle Trails Reference Map

Missouri Bicycle Trails Reference Map

Ohio Bicycle Trails Reference Map

Wisconsin Bicycle Trails Reference Map

State Trail Reference Maps & Guide Sets

Indiana Bicycle Trails Reference Map & Guide

Massachusetts Bicycle Trails Reference Map & Guide

Pennsylvania Bicycle Trails Reference Map & Guide

Virginia, Maryland, Delaware Bicycle Trails Reference Map & Guide

Books for the Recreational Bicyclist by

American Bike Trails

Illustrated Bicycle Trails Book Series

Illustrated bicycle trails throughout each state, in color and easy to reference and use. Includes directions to trail sites and accesses; with trail distances, general setting and conditions. State and sectional overviews, riding tips, locations and distances to nearby communities.

  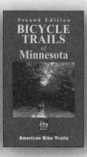  

Bicycle Trails of Illinois	Bicycle Trails of Iowa	Bicycle Trails of Minnesota	Mountain Bike Trails of Wisconsin	Recreatnl Bicycle Trails of Wisconsin
3rd Edition 2002	2nd Ed.	2nd Ed.	2nd Edition	ISBN 1-57430-102-0
ISBN 1-57430-113-6	ISBN 1-57430-115-2	ISBN 1-57430-090-3	ISBN 1-57430-025-3	122 pages 5 ½ x 9
160 pages	144 pages	144 pages	144 pages 5 ½ x 9	
5 ½ x 9	5 ½ x 9	5 ½ x 9		

Bicycle Trails & Ride Journal Book Series

Each spiral bound with spine (except for Illinois). Comprehensive descriptions of the many bicycle trails throughout each state covered. Details include riding tips, terms used, bicycle equipment tips, mileage chart, illustrations of trail locations, how to get there, length, uses, surface, setting and accessible facilities. All this in addition to an easy to use log for recording and referencing your rides.

Illinois Trails & Ride Journal	Indiana Trails & Ride Journal	Massa-chusetts Trails & Ride Journal	Mary-land Trails & Ride Journal	Pennsyl-vania Trails & Ride Journal	Virginia Trails & Ride Journal
ISBN 1-57430-114-4	ISBN 1-57430-116-0	ISBN 1-57430-120-9	ISBN 1-57430-122-5	ISBN 1-57430-118-7	ISBN 1-57430-124-1